Journals
as
Frameworks
for
Professional
Learning
Communities

Second Edition

Journals
as Frameworks for Professional Learning Communities

Second Edition

Mary E. Dietz

CORWIN PRESS
A SAGE Company
Thousand Oaks, CA 91320

For information:

Corwin Press
A SAGE Company
2455 Teller Road
Thousand Oaks, California 91320
www.corwinpress.com

SAGE Ltd.
1 Oliver's Yard
55 City Road
London, EC1Y 1SP
United Kingdom

SAGE India Pvt. Ltd.
B 1/I 1 Mohan Cooperative
Industrial Area
Mathura Road, New Delhi 110 044
India

SAGE Asia-Pacific Pte. Ltd.
33 Pekin Street #02-01
Far East Square
Singapore 048763

Printed in the United States of America

Library of Congress Cataloging-in-Publication Data

Dietz, Mary E.
  Journals as frameworks for professional learning communities / Mary E. Dietz. — 2nd ed.
    p. cm.
  Rev. ed. of: Journals as frameworks for change.
  Includes bibliographical references and index.
  ISBN 978-1-4129-5990-2 (cloth) — ISBN 978-1-4129-5991-9 (pbk.)
  1. Teachers—In-service training. 2. Teachers--Diaries. 3. Teachers—Professional relationships. 4. Portfolios in education. 5. Educational change. I. Dietz, Mary E. Journals as frameworks for change. II. Title.

  LB1731.D54 2008
  370.71'5—dc22

                                                        2007040300

This book is printed on acid-free paper.

07 08 09 10 11 10 9 8 7 6 5 4 3 2 1

Acquisitions Editor: Hudson Perigo
Editorial Assistants: Jordan Barbakow, Lesley Blake
Production Editor: Appingo Publishing Services
Cover Designer: Karine Hovsepian

Contents

Acknowledgments

I would like to take this opportunity to recognize the school communities that have contributed learnings reflected in the professional journals featured in this book: the New York City Teacher Centers Consortium; Acalanes High School District, Pleasant Hill, California; Travis Unified School District, Fairfield, California; Round Rock Independent School District, Austin, Texas; Aldine Independent School District, Houston, Texas; Long Beach Unified School District, Long Beach, California; and the California Beginning Teacher Support and Assessment programs. Through our shared experiences, we defined and refined the role of structured journals in facilitating and building capacities for learning communities.

—*Mary E. Dietz*

About the Author

Mary E. Dietz is an international consultant and former president and co-founder of LearnCity, a company dedicated to serving educators with a systemswide solution for designing, delivering, and assessing standards-based instruction using the power of technology.

 Ms. Dietz's career as a consultant began in 1989 when she established Frameworks for Learning Organizations. Prior to that she taught special education and served as a reading specialist for grades K–8. Her consulting practice is focused on assisting educational leaders in building their internal capacity for organizing and facilitating learning communities in school systems.

She has coached teachers, administrators, school boards, district and site leadership teams, and communities in establishing the collaborations and relationships necessary for systemic change. Much of her work with educators has been in the areas of systems design, strategic planning, professional development, coaching, and alternative assessments for educators.

Ms. Dietz is the founder of the National Staff Development Council's *Network for Portfolio Users* and is a member of the design team for establishing a Network for Educational Coaching in California. Most recently she served as the lead designer and facilitator in establishing an on line knowledge management system for implementing standards based instruction in California.

Introduction

THE PURPOSE OF PLC JOURNALS ■

Journals as Frameworks for Professional Learning Communities is designed as a resource for focusing and facilitating professional learning communities (PLCs). Districts and schools have a collection of professional structures such as site leadership teams, district leadership teams, school site councils, grade-level teams, subject matter instructional teams, professional development council, and principal's roundtable. They meet on a scheduled basis to accomplish an identified scope of work around a shared purpose and/or agreement. These networks, committees, and teams provide the structure and forum for professional work. Each time they meet, they have the opportunity to convene as a PLC. The following structured journals are tools that can focus and facilitate targeted work that could be in the scope of work for a given PLC:

- PLC journal—facilitating school reform
- Action research journal—teacher as researcher
- School portfolios—our school and its benefits
- Professional performance portfolio—highly qualified teacher
- PLC instructional planning—aligning professional development with instructional priorities

Each of these structured journals serves as a framework to focus and inform collaboration and learning and, ultimately, to improve student achievement. Journals are essential tools designed to focus and enhance learning for professional educators as they are utilized to support the work of PLCs. The real power is in the collection of PLCs working as a coherent and dynamic system to support student achievement. As educators and school community members come together, they share in a purpose and pursue deeper and broader understandings of their work. Working in PLCs and using the structured journal process, as outlined in this book, provides opportunities for learning community participants to reflect on and consider research and new practices that will impact student learning.

Senge (1990), who pioneered the concept of the learning community, invited educators to assist school communities in becoming learning organizations where they can encourage and support learning as part of their professional work. If knowledge is the capacity for effective action, educators have to ask how they can facilitate learning communities to support systemic change in their schools—by use of structured *Journals as Frameworks for Professional Learning Communities.*

■ HOW TO USE THIS BOOK AND CD

Journals as Frameworks for Professional Learning Communities begins with a chapter on journals and learning communities. This chapter describes the role of structured journals in supporting the process of building and sustaining learning communities. Subsequent chapters offer coaching guides for using the journaling process to facilitate each professional tool for addressing accountability mandates. These later chapters also help in enhancing teachers' repertoire for improved instructional practices through the collaborative and reflective processes structured in the journals for each of the professional activities (School Reform, Action Research, School Portfolio, Professional Performance, and Instructional Planning Journals).

Chapters begin with background on each journal and an explanation of *how* to use the structured journal to facilitate the process. See Figure 0.1 as a graphic representation of how journals can be used as frameworks for PLCs.

Featured in each chapter is a case study/sample journal illustrating the four-phase journaling process (purpose, focus, process, and outcome) that is applied for each journal.

Figure 0.1

Journals as Frameworks for PLCs

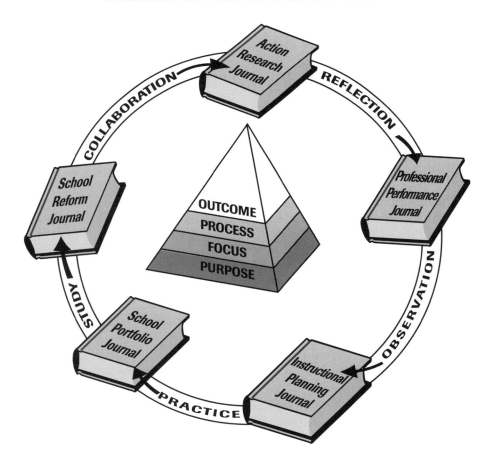

The case study constitutes an overview of the journaling process and offers completed journal pages and activities that are drawn from actual experiences with educators and school communities across the nation. The case study reveals how the journaling process is applied to facilitate thoughtful reflection, observation, study, practice, and collaboration. Following the case study is a wrap-up, which summarizes how to use the particular structured journal for the particular framework. Each chapter concludes with a wrap-up and helpful hints for implementation, a list of questions, and sentence stems that provide opportunities for discussion.

A resource section after Chapter 6 offers templates, implementation tools, strategies, and guides designed to assist learning community members in using the structured journal process. These resources are also found on the accompanying CD in addition to an MS Word© document file for each of the PLC Journals. The resource section concludes with a glossary of key terms, a bibliography that lists references and suggested readings on professional development as well as on building learning communities, and finally an index.

Before beginning this book and participating in the journaling, it is helpful to review the four principles on which this approach to professional learning is based. These principles form a backdrop for professional growth and collaboration as a learning community.

GUIDING PRINCIPLES FOR CONTINUOUS PROFESSIONAL LEARNING

Professional Learning Needs to Be Job Embedded—We Learn Through Our Work by Continually Expanding Our Repertoire

Professional development activities are most effective when professionals set their own goals, determine a preferred method for learning, and make decisions about how to best integrate new learnings (Krupp, 1991).

Professionals Learn by Experience and Opportunities to Engage in Reflective Collaborations With Peers

Professionals will engage in learning if they are involved in the process of discovering staff development (and collegial sharing) as a structure for change. This means that professionals will be empowered to build a plan that will support their goals as well as be encouraged to question current assumptions and explore new findings while gaining expertise and being responsible for agreed-upon outcomes (Glasser, 1993).

Collaboration Supports the Restructuring of Thinking and the Emergence of Professional Development

Professional growth is critical to the process of change in our schools (Joyce, 1990). Change is a process of resocialization that takes place over time and requires interaction. Partner meetings, peer with peer interaction, observation, and reflection are the most effective methods for initiating substantive change (Dietz, 1993).

Professionals Learn by Their Interactions With Colleagues, Observations, and New Ideas

The notion that we learn best when we are able to construct our own knowledge (constructivism) is a learning theory that has validity for adult learners. A school system can put this theory to practice and impact student learning by providing a) opportunities for coaching and expert assistance, b) an organizational structure that encourages teacher exchanges and observations, c) and has a performance system that acknowledges the principles of human development (M. G. Brooks & J. Grennon-Brooks, 1987).

■ THE LEARNING CYCLE OF PROFESSIONAL DEVELOPMENT

Use the "Learning Cycle" process to guide and deepen your level of engagement for peer-to-peer collaborations in the collection of journals found in this book.

Teachers Constructing Conceptual Understandings

Using a constructivist approach to teacher development allows teachers to experience the type of learning environment they are expected to create for their students. Two tools are helpful in focusing and facilitating this process: the Learning Cycle for Teacher Development and the Learner-Centered Coaching Model, both organized and facilitated by the professional development portfolio process.

The combination of these models allows teacher-learners to

1. clarify the purpose, meaning, and function of their work;

2. focus their learnings based on interests, concerns, and needs;

3. identify their current level of expertise regarding their focus for learning;

4. select an entry point for learning;

5. seek the appropriate coaching (collaboration) activities to support and facilitate their professional growth;

6. continually reflect on and self-assess their learnings;

7. describe, demonstrate, illustrate, or exhibit their refinements and learning outcomes.

This process can be used for beginning teachers and their mentors/coaches, or to support, in general, the professional development program for all teachers and their supervisors.

The Learning Cycle Model

The translation of learning theory into cycles of professional development is the foundation for the Learning Cycle Model. This model describes the pathway for continuous learning as teachers expand and deepen their understanding of the concepts and practices used in their profession. It helps teachers make informed decisions about appropriate learning plans for desired outcomes. Focusing learning in an effort to build conceptual understanding, the Learning Cycle Model assists teacher-learners in making connections among theories, practices, and their teaching experiences.

Judging by observation, research, and experience, it appears that teachers do pass through continuous learning cycles. These cycles are defined by four basic levels of development:

- **Exploration.** Teacher-learners are initially explorers, inquiring about a specific focus or priority. They are learning the territory, assessing information, observing students, listening to others, reading about theories, discovering new ideas, and exploring options and professional learning opportunities. Working with a mentor or coach, teacher-learners mediate their exploration by providing suggestions about professional development activities, asking questions, and sharing experiences.

- **Organization.** Teacher-learners observe as they (a) label things; (b) practice routines, procedures, and strategies; (c) clarify responses; and (d) recognize pedagogy and learning theories in their teaching environment. Representing what they have been observing and striving for, teacher-learners are prompted to place ideas in a sequence, accommodating and assimilating the data they have collected.

- **Connection.** Teacher-learners, having taken the initial exploration, organization, identification, and classification steps, transfer new ideas from one teaching-learning situation to another. The teacher-learners experiment with taking parts out of a neat, sequential order of lesson plans and modifying, altering, and integrating ideas. Ready to use for designing thematic units and facilitating collaboration regarding new ideas, these professional design plans feature strategies, techniques, and concepts from other lessons and/or content areas.

- **Reflection.** The teacher and the teaching profession are one. Teachers often make informed decisions without conscious thought, intuitively reflecting and responding. Teacher-learners in the Learning Cycle Model are in a reflective action mode while teaching, having learned to listen to the student and respond. What teacher-learners do consciously as connectors, they do naturally as reflectors.

The rate and sequence that teacher-learners move through this cycle is dependent on prior experiences and the motivational energy invested in learning. Learning is dependent on how prior experiences relate to the current set of circumstances. Learning is situational or contextual; therefore, the process, the plan, and the learner needs vary from individual to individual and from situation to situation.

The teachers and their mentors/coaches or colleagues engage in a structured interview (see the next section for model interview questions), which helps identify their current repertoire of knowledge, skills, values, and attitudes in the context of their priority area for learning. They then can move to the Learner-Centered Coaching Model, in which the teacher-learner and coach identify the most appropriate type of support and mediation for learning.

The Learner-Centered Coaching Model

Developing teachers need support, an infusion of knowledge, and opportunities to integrate learnings. They are dependent on their work (their colleagues, their students, and themselves) to provide the feedback necessary to become continual learners in their profession. The Learner-Centered Coaching Model is designed to assist these teacher-learners and their mentor/coaches, peers, or supervisors in determining where they are in their learning cycle, as well as what coaching behaviors would be most effective in facilitating continuous learning.

For learning to take place, several factors must be considered. The factors that influence learning are

- psychosocial/emotional development and well-being;
- experiential background—what has been observed and experienced;
- cognitive development—one's level of conceptual understanding and knowledge base.

These factors form a *learner profile* or frame of reference for an individual, profiling the interaction with the teacher's learning environment, which consists of

- the cognitive demands of the learning situation;
- the potential for emotional and/or aesthetic response; and
- the organization or structure for learning.

This *learning environment* provides the context or situation for development.

How the Learner-Centered Coaching Model Works

The Learner-Centered Coaching Model helps the coach (mentor) and teacher-learner collaborate to determine their needs in the professional growth process. The coach and the teacher-learner can then decide on the most effective coaching role or style for building the competence and commitment of the teacher. Using appropriate guidance and support should lead to teacher autonomy and efficacy.

Key contributors to determining where the learner is in terms of his or her learning cycle are

- levels of competence (experience and ability), and
- commitment (enthusiasm and willingness) in regard to the priority area for learning.

These key contributors should be explored in the context of factors that form the learner profile and learning environment. In the context of learning priority, these contributors can be determined by asking questions aimed at identifying the current knowledge, skills, values, and attitudes of the teacher-learners.

Suggested Interview Questions

The interviewer should supply the individual's selected portfolio priority or focus (represented by the blanks) as he or she poses these questions:

1. Describe how you _____.

2. How do you know if _____ is working?

3. What have you heard about or seen in regard to _____ that you would like to try?

4. What would you like to do, or do differently, as far as _____ is concerned?

5. How do you feel about where you are _____?

After exploring the individual's knowledge, skills, attitudes, and values, the teacher-learner, together with the coach, can decide where they are in their cycle and develop an appropriate learning plan. The level of direction for developing and implementing the plan can be determined by learning needs, facilitated by the portfolio journal process.

The coaches, peers, and/or supervisors can define their roles in response to the teacher-learner needs. The roles for coaching or guidance are advisor, planner, collaborator, and resource person.

- **Advisor.** This role is compatible with learners who are in the explorer phase of their cycle. They are beginning to discover, identify, observe, and gather experiences that will help them identify a priority for learning. The mentor/coach offers support and direction by making suggestions for discovery and exploration activities. He or she helps the teacher-learner identify and clarify issues that have emerged from experiences and observations.

- **Planner.** This role is compatible with teacher-learners who are moving into the organization phase of their learning cycle. They are starting to focus and identify a specific area for learning. As the teachers learn the terms, techniques, and successful practices related to their identified priority, the mentor/coaches help them clarify their focus and build a plan for organizing and implementing their learnings.

- **Collaborator.** This role is compatible with teacher-learners who are in the connection phase of their learning cycle. They have tried new practices and are at the point where they begin to modify, adapt, and transfer learnings into other areas of their professional practice. The mentor/coach works side by side with the teacher in planning, observing, implementing, and adapting new practices. Often new ideas and suggestions emerge from these two-way, collaborative conversations.

- **Resource person.** This role is compatible with teacher-learners who are at the reflection phase of their learning cycle, that is, in a targeted area of learning. Teacher-learners have internalized new ideas and made decisions to use these new practices while actively teaching. The coach is a resource, available for support, guidance, or feedback when the teacher calls for it.

All four roles enlist varying measures of support and direction based on learner needs. Thus the proper amount of psychological support, direction, and knowledge-building experiences necessary to assist the teacher can be identified. Coaches or mentors continually adapt their roles in the learning process to match the needs of the teacher-learners. This methodology facilitates continuous learning and reflection on learnings. Providing closure in the inquiry process as the learner completes the cycle, the Learner-Centered Coaching Model facilitates the professional development portfolio process and identifies a new priority for learning.

Summary of the Learning Cycle

The Learner-Centered Coaching Model has been used successfully with both beginning and veteran teachers. The following benefits have been observed:

- Focused learning—allowing for deeper levels of understanding
- Alignment between the individual teacher's goals and those of the school
- Clear definition of the role of coach, peer, mentor, or supervisor
- Transfer of learning-to-learn principles to the classroom
- Increased impact of professional development activities
- Contribution to building a collegial culture in the school community
- Practicing of collaboration techniques
- Eagerness to learn from experiences
- Integration of learning and assessment models (best practices) in the classroom

Figure 0.2

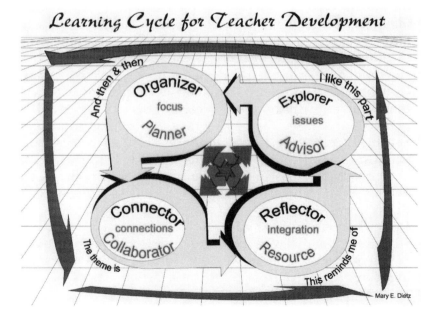

Learning Cycle for Teacher Development

— Mary E. Dietz

LEARNING COMMUNITIES READINESS RUBRIC ■

Knowledge and Abilities

1) Leadership is viewed as a behavior and is shared among team members.

strongly agree	agree	disagree	strongly disagree
4	3	2	1

2) Knowledge of the nature of adult learning is understood and applied.

strongly agree	agree	disagree	strongly disagree
4	3	2	1

3) Awareness of constructivist learning theory—that we learn by interacting with people, objects, and ideas—is evidenced in our work.

strongly agree	agree	disagree	strongly disagree
4	3	2	1

4) Understanding of systems, that we are interdependent and part of the evolving big picture, and that we all contribute to our outcomes.

strongly agree	agree	disagree	strongly disagree
4	3	2	1

5) We practice effective communication skills such as active listening to learn, to ask questions, and to understand.

strongly agree	agree	disagree	strongly disagree
4	3	2	1

6) We understand the dynamics of change an consider them in designing and facilitating implementation plans.

strongly agree	agree	disagree	strongly disagree
4	3	2	1

7) We continually expand and refine our knowledge base related to the context of our work.

strongly agree	agree	disagree	strongly disagree
4	3	2	1

8) We practice effective facilitation skills to provide structure and enhance the process of focusing and organizing our work.

strongly agree	agree	disagree	strongly disagree
4	3	2	1

Knowledge and Ability Development Levels

16 or less   Frustration level

17 to 23   Awareness and learning

24 to 27   Partial integration into work environment

28 to 32   Infused into the work culture

(Lev Vygotsky ZONE of Proximal Development)

Commitments and Attitudes

1) We respect the diversity of others.

strongly agree	agree	disagree	strongly disagree
4	3	2	1

2) There is a willingness to suspend assumptions and avoid jumping to conclusions without first communicating directly.

strongly agree	agree	disagree	strongly disagree
4	3	2	1

3) We honor our history and respect ground rules/norms for working together.

strongly agree	agree	disagree	strongly disagree
4	3	2	1

4) We ask questions to understand the intentionality of actions and comments.

strongly agree	agree	disagree	strongly disagree
4	3	2	1

5) We accept feedback recognizing that learning is a vital contributor to continuous improvement.

strongly agree	agree	disagree	strongly disagree
4	3	2	1

6) We are committed to making learning communities a priority.

strongly agree	agree	disagree	strongly disagree
4	3	2	1

7) We are open minded and pose essential (big idea) questions to stimulate thinking and broaden our scope of possibilities.

strongly agree	agree	disagree	strongly disagree
4	3	2	1

8) We are flexible and accept that certainty is a myth and that in an evolving system there is constant change.

strongly agree	agree	disagree	strongly disagree
4	3	2	1

Commitment and Attitude Readiness Levels

16 or less	Direction to begin process
17 to 23	Coaching and mediation to learn and practice
24 to 27	Support and follow-up to sustain progress
28 to 32	Checkpoints to maintain and continually improve

(Adapted from Situational Leadership: the connection between the leadership and membership in an organization in regard to the ratio of willingness and ability to learn and continually improve)

Professional Learning Communities at Work

We seek meaning and significance from building purposeful communities. (Sergiovanni, 1994, p. xiii).

BUILDING LEARNING COMMUNITIES IN SCHOOLS ■

Clusters of learning communities form a learning organization when an organization, as a whole, commits to learn continually from and about its work. Today many organizations are learning disabled: the norms of the organization inhibit learning from its work. For instance, a school whose professional development program is task-orientated rather than purpose-orientated forces the organization members into a narrow focus, which does not invite continuous growth.

In terms of working with learning communities in schools, there seems to be a direct relationship between success with continuous improvement efforts and a school community in which learning is a valued part of the professional practice and conversations among staff members.

Tom Sergiovanni (1994) suggested that the desire for community is part of human nature and a basic need. He believed that because no cookie-cutter recipe for community building exists, each school will have to invent its own practice of community. Sergiovanni also acknowledged, "[W]e humans seek meaning and significance above all, and building purposeful communities helps us find both" (p. 95).

It seems logical that having such an organization in school communities would be ideal. Educators might even assume that schools already *are* learning communities. Unfortunately, that is not the case. The lack of learning communities might even be a key contributor for the reason why so many school reform efforts have failed. In order to address the urgent needs of our educational process and define the purpose of schooling in the Information Age, we must create an environment where learning *and* constructing new ideas are an expected part of the daily practice of professional educators: a place where all can work together to challenge past practices and work toward a shared purpose defined by professional collaboration and learning.

The teaching profession is being redefined at a rapid rate by the changing needs and purposes of education for today's youngsters and communities. In working with the Teacher Centers in the New York City Public Schools and with other school systems, as a facilitator, I noted that educators are focused on identifying attributes of being a professional educator in the twenty-first century. The educators recognize that if their work is to support and contribute to the growth of the teaching profession in the future, they must consider the essential attributes of a professional teacher.

Working with the professional development portfolio and other frameworks for change, I found the following essential attributes or mind-sets of a professional teacher emerged:

1. *Do no harm.* As a special education teacher, I interviewed students when they entered my program. I would ask, "When did you begin to believe you could not learn in school?" They could *always* tell me. They knew the circumstances, the teacher, and the event that convinced them that "*I cannot be successful here.*"

   As professionals, we must create a learning environment for students that encourages and nurtures whatever level of intelligence or maturity nature has provided them. We must provide a true learning environment of coaching for all of our students no matter where they are able to enter the learning process.

2. *Be an informed visionary.* So often, teachers are asked to adopt another's vision or purpose of schooling. Each teacher *must* have his or her own commitment to the purpose of education and dedication to cultivating and expanding each student's repertoire of understanding. To do this, educators must possess professional skills, know how individuals learn, know how the brain works, and know the critical juncture points of a child's social and emotional development. With that background, professionals can add content and instructional practices that assist students in constructing their own personal understandings and expanding their knowledge.

3. *Inform others.* How many times have you gone to the doctor's office and really appreciated it when the doctor took the time to explain what is happening with your body as well as the anticipated effects of a prescribed treatment? It is the same with the teaching profession. Educators need to inform themselves and their communities of the research, individual discoveries, and professional

experiences that have informed and enlightened their practices. Parents always feel appreciative and more in control when they understand what is happening in the school environment as their children develop.

For example, there is a time in the development of a young child's visual system when reversals of letters might occur when she or he is reading. Usually this lasts for a short period as the brain routes and solidifies new connections. Sometimes reversal of letters is an indicator of a more complex problem such as a perceptional disability or dyslexia. Observation and time will determine whether the exhibited phenomenon is a phase or an indicator of something else. When parents understand this, they are willing to watch and wait with the teacher as they all observe, collaborate, and facilitate the child's developing skills.

4. *Every child is unique.* Educators must always remember that each child presents a new situation. Each child is unique in physical, emotional, social, and intellectual gifts and requires customized attention. This uniqueness celebrates and challenges professional decision making as teachers determine the best materials and practices to maximize learning and development for that child. This uniqueness also explains why "covering the curriculum" does not necessarily mean most students in a class have added to their knowledge base.

These four attributes share the need for continuous professional collaborative research and learning on the part of teachers.

The Nature of a Learning Organization and Learning Communities

A learning organization is not a building that breathes but rather a collection of community members who give life, presence, flexibility, adaptability, responsiveness, new thinking, and energy to their organization and the work it does. A learning organization is a collection of learning communities—small groups organized around individuals' work and shared purposes. The efforts of each learning community within the learning organization contribute to the coevolving, living system (Capra, 1982), which is the learning organization. The organization is dependent on learning communities to sustain it and help it grow. Learning communities infuse new thinking and suggestions for improvement into the organization, which would not exist without the collection of learning communities within the system.

Why Are Learning Communities Needed in Schools?

The breakneck speed of change in the information age has educators reeling and continually adapting and accommodating to the changing needs in our world. Learning communities allow for establishing norms of adjustment to change by continually infusing new thinking and practices into the work and accommodating changes and supporting community members through transitions. Peter Block (1993) commented, "If there is not transformation inside of us, all the structural change in the world will have no impact on our institutions" (p. 77).

Learning communities invite the conversations, feedback, and risk taking necessary for individual transformation and systemic changes. Altering a structure alone does not necessarily mean systemic change will occur.

For example, faculties in several high schools in California, going through a restructuring process, learned that block scheduling was a structural change that had little impact on student learning if teachers did not change their professional practices. The educators in the decision-making process agreed that the purpose of the block scheduling was to improve student learning by increasing the use of interactive, interdisciplinary practices. It was also agreed that block schedules could consolidate subject matter and help students focus on just a few subjects at a time, deepening their understanding of the concepts embedded in the content. Furthermore, by spending more time with fewer teachers, students would seem to have more opportunities to build a sense of community in class.

As the process for change continued, some of the school faculties chose to vote on whether to have block scheduling. Interestingly enough, those teachers who were forced to participate in the change to block scheduling simply did in ninety minutes what they had always done in forty-five minutes. On reexamination of those classrooms wherein the instructors were forced to implement block scheduling, it was found there was no change in fundamental teaching practices or student outcomes.

Another example of how changes in structures alone will not necessarily make a difference is the decision to use site-based management (SBM), as explored by a group of schools in New York. When shared decision making and SBM schools were considered by a group of district personnel, many of the school principals in the group seemed aligned in theory with the process, but only as long as they still had veto power over decisions. However, teachers who came to the table as part of the process were very much interested in decision-making power regarding hirings and budget allocations. So a roomful of people were negotiating for shared governance. The conversations were not about how student learning could be improved but about power. Participants were operating off an old paradigm and altering the structure did nothing to alter the conditions.

Over time, however, the conversations began to evolve into asking about purpose and about how SBM could help achieve that purpose. The team facilitators began asking questions: What do we need to know about shared decision making? What do *we* want for *our* school? As team members became willing to listen and learn, they began building their understandings and abilities resulting in a change in their attitudes toward the process, thus contributing toward a shared purpose as a school community. Through the process of questioning, individuals had shifted their power and purpose; change was actually achieved in a meaningful way.

Who Is in a Learning Community?

Members of a learning community are individuals with *diverse* philosophies, experiences, expertise, and personalities. Within a school community, learning communities can and do include members inside and outside the walls of the school building, as shown in Figure 1.1. The community-at-large is responsible for the educational process of youngsters; therefore, building learning communities composed of all parties involved in the educational process is critical. Professional educators come to their work with varying values, skills, knowledge bases, and beliefs. Their first and foremost challenge is to align their needs and purposes with those of the entire community. All learning community members are part of the critical life force of the organization. Their collaborations, interactions, and shared understandings are the life force that energizes and connects individuals and forms cohesive learning communities. Through working together, the individuals recognize their interdependence and the richness in their diversity. Learning communities in schools should include children, educators, parents, business partners, and other organizations in the community that contribute to the schooling process.

One school in southern California was experiencing great divisiveness among staff and community. The community was demanding changes in the school, focusing on staff development practices and the lack of equity in the bussing process. The conversations in parent group meetings became heated and, at times, ugly. The school leadership decided to have a community night and redesign the process of using parent opinions and desires in the decision-making process at the school.

Figure 1.1   Members of the Learning Community Working Toward Change

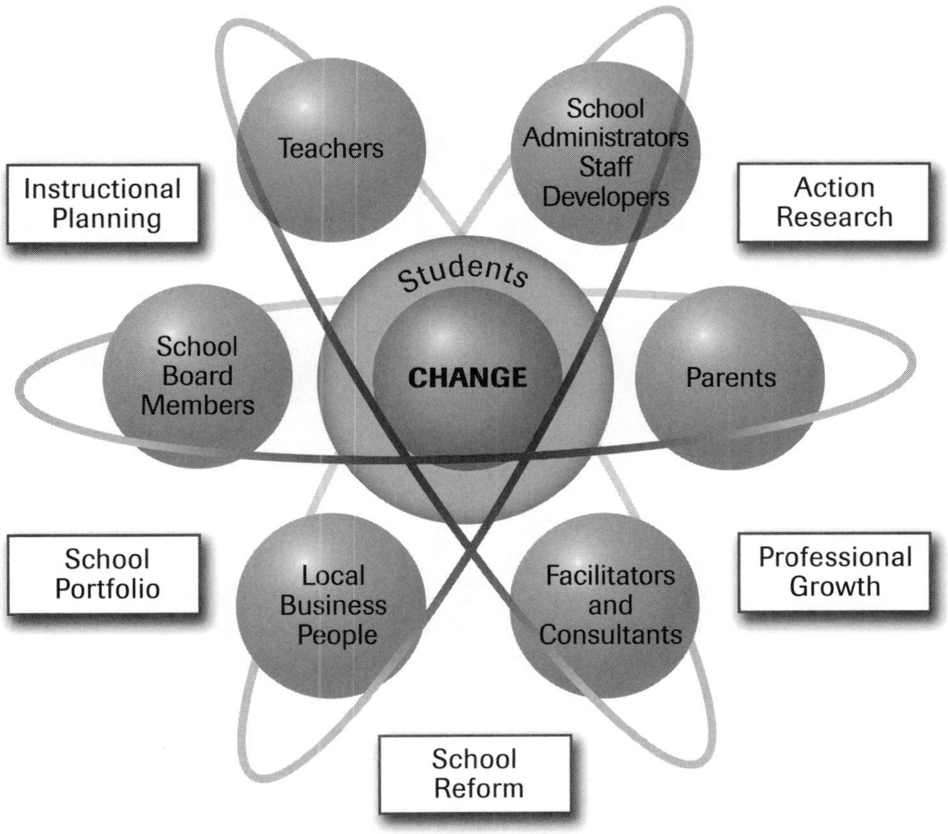

The first step in the process was to reconstruct the history of the school. Community members were invited to join the staff for an evening to tell the story of their school. They recounted changes that had occurred in curriculum, staff, student enrollment, assessments, and physical structures. Working in decade groups, the participants recounted the history of the school from the decade in which it opened to the 1990s. After a representative from each group summarized the highlights of that particular decade, everyone looked for outstanding achievements in which they felt pride. Group participants then discussed what to keep and the lessons that had been learned.

Drawing from the experience of that evening, the group began to set a new purpose and priorities for the school. For each priority, they formed an action team which included a school staff member. Community members were invited to participate on a team that addressed one of their greatest interests or concerns. Several staff members and parents attended facilitation-training sessions and were willing to serve as team facilitators. The action teams met monthly and developed a plan with both short- and long-term goals. The first "community night" meeting was in 1994, and to this day, the learning community process established that night still serves that school community as they work together to address the challenge of educating children.

■ THE IMPORTANCE OF CONVERSATION AND BUILDING RELATIONSHIPS

Building relationships is at the heart of learning communities. The reciprocal process of *colearning* fuels the continued growth and vitality within the community. Members of a learning community are committed to continually improving their efforts and refining their practices on an ongoing basis. They are willing and able to move out of isolation and engage in collegial (professional) conversations about their work.

School communities as well as communities-at-large are experiencing complex problems that are not easily resolved. Some have referred to these problems as falling into one of two categories: wicked problems and tame problems. Wicked problems are complex and not easily definable. There are no existing algorithms for solving wicked problems, and they are iterative in nature; that is, the problems are recursive and continually evolving. Tame problems, on the other hand, are definable. The boundaries of involvement and areas for intervention appear clear. There are existing algorithms. Today schools and communities are facing greater numbers of wicked problems that are not effectively solved with an easy answer. These problems are multidimensional and self-generating and require continual attention and adaptations (Bailey, 1996).

Members of learning communities put meaning into their work by defining a common purpose and function. The emphasis in a learning community is on building commitment, not on constructing compliant structures. The environment is one of shared responsibility rather than managerial accountability. In these times of wicked problems, there is an increased need to work together and to be open to new ideas and new solutions. When solutions are mandated solutions, forced upon the organization from the outside, there is little possibility for building commitment for implementation of shared solutions nor for willingness to continually revisit the effectiveness of the mandated solution over time.

ESSENTIAL QUALITIES AND ROLES OF ■ LEARNING COMMUNITY MEMBERS

In a learning community, individual members are both *learners* and *leaders* who are willing to suspend assumptions, respect the ideas of others, and engage in dialogue to continually construct and refine their purpose and shared understandings. As members take responsibility for learning and leading together, they build new understandings of leadership and leadership actions. Learning community members are *adaptive, generative,* and *creative* with their practices. They are committed to continually improving their work by engaging in reflective collaborations. They seek new ideas, feedback, and opportunities to reflect and collaborate. Members are leaders who take action to generate new thinking and construct new designs for their work.

Each individual member is an integral part of a dynamic, evolving system. The system as a whole is greater than the sum of the parts. Synergy exists. In a learning community, there is recognition of members' interdependence and a reciprocal process of learning. Each member is committed to infusing new ideas, rethinking existing structures, and reflecting on experiences. As members interact (with people, events, and ideas) and reflect on their experiences, each person contributes to the evolving process of the learning community and its members.

Members of learning communities establish trusting relationships by clearly articulating intentions and purposes. Relationships are formed with respect, honesty, and professional ethics. Collegiality builds among members as they clarify their intentions and identify assumptions to avoid misunderstandings. Members recognize how the flow of information and the dynamics of learning are disrupted when faulty assumptions are made regarding intentions.

Learning communities invite the whole person. Community members nourish and enhance the ongoing cognitive, experiential, and emotional development of learning community members (Dietz, 1994).

This happens through the interactions, trust building, and hard work aimed toward a shared purpose. Structures or frameworks such as action research and school reform groups offer openings to build relationships that invite shared learning.

Ongoing relationships generate energy and cohesiveness in order to facilitate and sustain the learning system's communities. Wheatley (1992) stated that relationships are key in supporting systemic change. She pointed out, "[W]e do not really know who we are until we enter into a relationship with another" (p. 44). It is only during the relationship-building stage that people are challenged to define who they are, what they do, and their contribution to an organization.

Learning communities are formed one conversation at a time, through reflection and interaction with others about their experiences, ideas, and purposes. Members increase their capacity to listen, to dialogue, and to construct new understandings. Increased trust and knowledge of shared purpose enable members to make decisions for the good of the learning community, which in turn serves the good of individuals. Members recognize the ultimate benefits of finding common ground and respect each other's contribution to achievements.

Members of learning communities work toward agreement of both purpose and actions to fulfill that purpose. Each member assumes leadership roles and takes leadership actions as appropriate (Lambert et al., 1995). Learning communities need members who

- facilitate conversations and decision making;
- acknowledge the history, norms, and pride in the organization;
- support members through the disequilibrium of change;
- accept responsibility for the learning of self and of others in the organization.

Members of learning communities learn from their work and from each other. They welcome opportunities to invent meaningful and purposeful staff development experiences and continually refine their practice. Accepting their responsibility to stay informed about new practices and research that applies to their work, learning community members are mindful of their commitment to improve continually and support each other in redesigning and modifying their professional behaviors.

■ FACILITATING LEARNING COMMUNITIES

Learning communities are groups of individuals who have come together with a shared purpose and agree to construct new understandings…a place where people continually expand their capacity to create the results they truly desire, where new and expansive patterns of thinking are nurtured, where collective aspiration is set free, and where people are continually learning how to learn together. (Senge, 1990, p. 14)

Building a sense of community within a group, a learning community starts with relationships and evolves one conversation at a time. Relationships grow when there is a framework or structure for conversation, work, and reflection; when there is a commitment to building the capacity to have meaningful, focused conversations; and when there is a recognition and commitment on the part of members. Building relationships is a critical factor that influences the impact of the group members' learnings on their professional work.

Frameworks for PLC, and the use of the journal process within those frameworks, are helpful in supporting and sustaining learning communities. Following are three examples of how people working together in learning communities can achieve school improvement through such frameworks:

- *Action research.* A group of first-grade teachers study assessment strategies and use their classrooms to evaluate which system will help them best demonstrate student progress.

- *School reform.* A PLC serving as a site leadership team (SLT) meets regularly as a team and periodically with the entire faculty to agree on instructional priorities. The SLT facilitates the process to (1) analyze student data and agree on instructional priorities, (2) determine professional development needs, (3) implement an action plan, and (4) monitor progress.
- *Professional Development for Instructional Priorities.* A PLC or grade level team makes a commitment to review student data and align their professional development with identified instructional priorities. They agree to generate essential questions regarding their current practices and pursue an inquiry process, which leads them to understanding the gaps in their programs and identifying instructional priorities for change. This PLC process informs their decisions regarding professional development priorities for targeting student achievement by implementing new instructional practices. They learn about new instructional practices and programs to address specific instructional needs of students. They monitor progress and make adjustments as indicated.

Members of learning communities build capacity by developing knowledge, skills, and attitudes that will help them grow professionally. Professional development is achieved through experiences with constructivist leadership, knowledge of adult learning, and awareness of constructivist learning theory. Drawn from an understanding of systems, communication abilities, and acceptance of the dynamics of change, facilitation skills are essential to focus and organize a learning community.

Attitudes and attributes that support learning communities include

- respect for diversity of others and willingness to suspend assumptions;
- honor of another's history and respect of cultural norms;
- willingness to seek understanding of others' intentions;
- willingness to listen and learn;
- openness to posing and responding to essential questions;
- recognition of the vital role of learning communities;
- acceptance that certainty is a myth;
- commitment to making learning communities a priority.

Many school systems around the world have begun to assess the condition of their school communities. Teachers within those systems and other school community members, seeking to establish themselves as learning organizations, are looking for a way to begin the process of change. The vision of transforming schools into learning organizations provides a cohesive and agile framework for educators beginning the twenty-first century. Because of this vision, there is a new paradigm for schools: learner-centered instruction, purposeful learning, and continual improvement of professional practices.

2

Professional Learning Community Journal

Facilitating School Reform

BACKGROUND OF PROFESSIONAL ■
LEARNING COMMUNITIES

A professional learning community (PLC) provides a collaborative environment for teachers, administrators, other school staff, parents, and community members—with their varying backgrounds, knowledge, and skills—to come together to learn. It offers a learning environment for members to agree upon a shared purpose and a process for working and learning together to accelerate student achievement. In some districts, PLCs have become part of the fabric of the culture. Professional development planning and learning opportunities are structured around PLCs. Often PLCs function as site leadership teams (SLTs) whose primary purpose in a school community is to examine the current state of student success and to explore and consider educational practices that will result in an increase in student achievement.

PLCs can create innovations to minimize or avoid the traditional compliance-implementation process. The group provides time for members to explore theoretical backgrounds and to reflect on teaching practices, constructing a framework for thoughtfully planned innovation and implementation.

As an example of what a PLC can accomplish, a PLC serving as an SLT in a large, urban school district recently formed PLCs to

- assist in implementing curricular and instructional innovations;
- develop school improvement plans;
- give impetus to a focus on instructional innovations and successful practices in terms of teaching and learning.

A Structured Journal Supports the PLC With School Improvement Planning

Portfolios and structured journals can be used to support, document, facilitate, and assess learning. Over the years, educators have used portfolios with structured journals for many purposes. The power of the portfolio is that, by design, the portfolio process can accommodate varying purposes from accountability for progress and performance to facilitating and supporting professional learning. In the era of No Child Left Behind (NCLB), high school reform, and interventions for low-performing schools, the portfolio structure and process serve as a guide and container for organizing, focusing, monitoring, and reporting change.

For example, the PLC school reform portfolio can support the PLC that is serving as an SLT for instructional improvement and include all stakeholders. The PLC school reform journal supports the work of instructional improvement with a systems approach to action planning. A systems approach combined with shared decision making, lateral leadership, and a shared purpose of all involved is foundational to this work—the work of coming together as a PLC, serving as an SLT, and preparing to focus on instructional priorities for student achievement. The following shows how the portfolio process can serve the systems approach to school reform efforts and the relationship-building process to promote sustainable changes. A PLC school reform portfolio process can be organized around four dynamic phases for a comprehensive learning process:

1. **Purpose.** Bring key stakeholders together such as an SLT to define their shared purpose for improvement and make commitments to research "study" instructional practices aligned with their instructional priorities aimed at accelerating student achievement with measurable outcomes.

2. **Focus.** Use a systems planning model to focus work and identify urgent instructional priorities. We have a great many tools and intervention programs; the question is how we can use a planning model, in the PLC school reform journal, to identify the best entry point for change in the school system. Structures such as the SLT can be an established professional learning community with a commitment to getting the results key stakeholders have agreed upon. The SLT meets at regularly scheduled times to
   - analyze student data to identify targeted instructional priority;
   - assess current capacity and teacher readiness for achieving their student achievement goal;

- build knowledge and skills necessary to achieve the targeted instructional goal;
- research best practices that address the school's identified instructional priorities;
- strategize for building capacity for successful implementation of new instructional strategies.

3. **Process.** Design and implement the action plan, inviting all stakeholders to participate in planning, implementing, monitoring, and reporting results. Collect artifacts and evidence of progress as well as lessons learned to share and archive as part of the commitment to a systems approach for action planning.

4. **Outcomes.** Demonstrate and articulate results. Look into the future with next steps using the archived tools, structures, and outcomes (see Figure 2.1).

Figure 2.1   Systems Planning Model

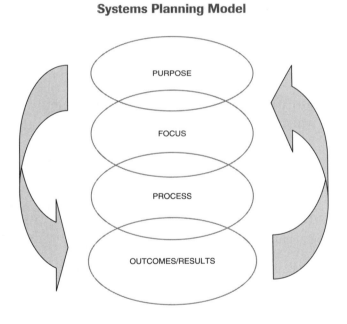

Systems Planning Model

Multilevels of Planning for Results

Planning is a process, not just a document. Thus, focusing on the organization and process of planning as a continuous progression guides a community of learners to their agreed-upon outcomes. Table 2.1 describes the planning model to assist with organizing the phases, activities, tools, and structures for designing, facilitating, implementing, refining, and sustaining school reform.

Table 2.1   Organizers for the Systems Planning Model

PORTFOLIO JOURNAL PHASE	KEY ACTIVITIES	TOOLS AND STRUCTURES
Purpose for work	• Clarify purpose and how SLT will serve school reform purpose • Obtain leadership and Sponsorship for the work • Engage key stakeholders • Define roles and responsibilities	• Alignment on purpose • Establish Site Leadership Team (SLT) • Orient SLT to the Systems Planning Model and the Journal Process • Facilitation strategies
Focus for priorities	• Facilitate staff meetings to introduce process • Establish process for data analysis • Agree on instructional priorities in grade-level or subject-matter work teams	• Instructional priority setting process • Engage staff in data analysis and establishing an instructional priority • Engage faculty in identifying professional development needs to build capacity for instructional priority
Process for planning and monitoring progress	• Build action plan to implement new instructional practices • Establish professional development plan for implementing new instructional practices • Schedule check points to monitor progress	• Implement action plan and monitor progress • Implement professional development activities • Establish checkpoints with protocols • Collect learnings with artifacts and evidence of progress • Make adjustments in action plan according to check-point data
Outcomes for reporting results	• Assess and articulate results • Debrief lessons learned and impact of new practices • Report results to stakeholders • Decide next steps • Celebrate accomplishments	• Reflect on learnings from the process • Draw conclusions on results • Refine and archive collection of artifacts and evidence for reporting result

*These Key Activities are the most critical elements for establishing a sound foundation and organization to build the capacity and support the change process for school reform. These key activities contribute to building a professional learning community.

HOW TO USE THE PLC SCHOOL REFORM ■
JOURNAL TO INFORM PLANNING

As with the other structured journals, the PLC school reform journal process involves four phases (purpose, focus, process, and outcome). A PLC serving as an SLT is typically comprised of the teacher-leaders who facilitate and direct the school reform process at their school site. The members of the SLT, drawn from school faculty and leadership, first meet to discuss their purpose and function, their role and responsibilities, and specifically, their targeted priority for working together. Part of this phase involves determining how members of the SLT will work together as well as norms, protocols, and, particularly, the results or expected outcomes of their work.

In the case of the SLT mentioned previously—the one that serves as the focus of the case study in this chapter—the professional portfolio process had been used as an alternative teacher evaluation in the past. The school district decided, that considering the success of the portfolio structured journal process in the past they would apply the PLC school reform journal process for the SLT, using a systems approach to school reform and action planning to improve student achievement.

As this SLT met for the second session, it devoted time to determining its targeted instructional priority. Using the four-phase process, participants analyzed multiple sources of student data to begin to agree on instructional priorities for action planning, their focus to support their school improvement plan. Instructional priorities were determined based on analysis of student data. The SLT decided that the next best step would be to work in grade-level teams to identify next steps to research successful practices, formative assessments, and differentiated instructional models for their instructional priority.

The next few meetings were sessions in which members of the learning community reflected on their data analysis and research of successful practices for their instructional priority as they began to prepare for their next faculty-wide meeting to engage the entire staff in the discussion regarding the action planning process to address their instructional priority. As they continued through the four-phase process and implemented their action plan, SLT members facilitated regular "checkpoint" sessions with the faculty to monitor progress with their instructional priority and to make adaptations in the plan as indicated. The final session was devoted to presenting outcomes and the results regarding student performance and to reflecting their work as an SLT, facilitating the process and supporting professional growth.

Organization

The PLC school reform journal, being organized around the four phases (purpose, focus, process, and outcome), guides and facilitates the group in the chosen area of research and inquiry.

The PLC members begin by clarifying what an SLT is, why they are part of it, and what they would like to accomplish. Critical questions to address at this initial step include the following:

- What is your primary purpose for participating in the SLT?
- What will your SLT commitment be in terms of participation and contributions?
- How will your SLT support your work with your instructional priority?

Journal Process and Design

Journaling facilitates collaboration and reflection. The journal forms in this chapter will assist in using a systems approach to action planning to improve student achievement.

Why? (Purpose)

- As an SLT, orient yourselves to the process.
- Identify team membership, roles, and responsibilities.
- Clarify your primary purpose and how you will serve school reform at your school site.

What? (Focus)

- Facilitate staff meetings to introduce a process for grade-level or department teams to meet and analyze student data.
- Analyze multiple sources of student data to identify instructional priorities, the focus of your SLT school reform work.
- Determine instructional strategies to be employed and professional development needs to prepare for implementation.

How? Action Planning (Process)

- Review the action plan with faculty for final agreement.
- Set up professional development schedule to implement new instructional strategies.
- SLT members and instructional coaches support grade-level teams with implementation of new instructional strategies.
- Schedule "checkpoints" to monitor progress and make adaptations in the plan as indicated.
- Collect evidence of progress.

So What? (Outcome)

- Assess and articulate results.
- Report results to school community-at-large.
- Debrief lessons learned regarding the process and the impact on professional development and student achievement.
- Celebrate accomplishments and identify next steps.

When the school reform process is introduced as a structure and process for professional learning and collaboration, SLT members agree that the focus for their collaborative work will be directly aligned with student achievement and addressing their school's instructional priority. See "The Learning Cycle of Professional Development" section in the Introduction to assist in determining the current level of understanding or readiness for implementing new instructional strategies. This process can support the professional development design and process for building capacity to expand teacher's repertoire.

CASE STUDY: PLC SCHOOL REFORM JOURNAL ■

Following is an overview of the journaling process including samples of journals and activities from actual PLC experiences. When you are ready to apply the PLC school reform journaling process with your colleagues, note that the journal templates of the PLS school reform journal forms shown here are offered at the end of this chapter and on the accompanying CD. Commentary is provided before each sample form explaining how the SLT in this case applied the structured journal process to facilitate their school reform process.

The visual and accompanying table of activities represents a systems planning model. The systems planning model is directly aligned with the four phases of the structures journal process.

The questions in the first journal form—Why? (Purpose) involve initial observations and reflections by individual participants regarding the purpose of the SLT (see Figure 2.2). Reflection and observation are strategies integral to the purpose step of the process.

Figure 2.2   Why? (Purpose)

PURPOSE • COMMITMENT• GOALS

1. From my point of view the primary purpose of our site leadership team is the following:

    In my school community, it seems that there is a growing conflict between a traditional top-down approach to managing our work and a growing need to move into a shared leadership focused on improved student achievement. With so many changes I think having an SLT could give us an opportunity to work collectively as a school community focused on student learning and making decisions together to achieve our shared priority instructional goals.

2. I bring the following expertise and commitment to our team efforts:

    I have been a fifth-grade teacher at this school for six years and have an expertise in reading and supporting English language learners. I am committed to working on engaging all our faculty in the process of agreeing on what is best for the students and supporting their academic success.

3. I will consider our site leadership team efforts a success if the following things happen this year:

    1. The staff attains agreement on priority instructional goals.

    2. We share our expertise regarding successful practices and support each other in improving academic performance of our students.

    3. We make a commitment to continue our work as a team.

As the PLC school reform structured journal process continues, the SLT focuses on identifying their instructional priority. The What? (Focus) journal form (see Figure 2.3) introduces the process that the faculty will follow to determine their instructional priority, the focus for their work. At this point, the SLT engages the faculty in understanding the process for analyzing student data to determine their instructional priority. They establish rapport with the faculty and clarify roles and responsibilities such as the role of grade-level teams in supporting the schoolwide effort as they move through the process. It is important to realize that the successful outcomes of this effort are dependent on building trusting relationships from the start with frequent and honest communications. Checking out the resource section of this book and accompanying CD and considering the use of some of the facilitation tool may be helpful—for example, to the levels of listening and to listening to understand. This is helpful in beginning, especially when SLT members are still calibrating their roles and faculty members are trying to understand the process and how it could support their work.

At this point, SLT moves from the purpose and focus phases to using the How Will It Work? Action Planning (Process) journal form (see Figure 2.4)—the SLT constructs the action plan for achieving successful outcomes with their instructional priority. The SLT reviews the action plan with the faculty for final agreement and begins the professional

Figure 2.3   What? Instructional Priorities (Focus)

DATA • ANALYSIS • PRIORITIES

As an SLT, facilitate a staff meeting where each grade level or department shares its priority area for instructional improvement.

At a staff meeting, we introduced our four-phase process for determining instructional priority goals. We brought samples of student data to practice the data analysis process. We also set up a second session where we reported out, by grade level, areas we were considering for instructional improvement.

Four-phase data analysis process for determining instructional priority:

1. Organize multiple sources of student data in grade-level and/or department teams.

2. Include standardized tests scores, program/publisher tests, classroom-generated tests, samples of student work and observations.

3. Analyze data student data and look for patterns, themes, and compelling "Ahas."

As a staff, we determined that one area of instructional improvement all grade levels had in common was reading comprehension. For our first pass as working as a staff on instructional priorities, we decided to make reading comprehension a schoolwide priority.

4. The goal is to agree on two to three instructional priorities for the year.

Figure 2.4   How? Action Planning (Process)

PLAN • LEARN • IMPLEMENT • MONITOR

Action Plan Table

The following table describes the planning model to assist with organizing the phases, activities, tools, and structures to design, facilitate, implement, and sustain school reform.

PHASE	PARTICIPANTS	KEY ACTIVITIES
PURPOSE PLC Serving as an SLT	SLT—School administrator and teacher representing multigrade levels and specializations in the school	1. Determine SLT membership 2. Define SLT purpose, roles, and responsibilities 3. Set up dates and times for SLT meetings and for faculty meetings 4. Establish dates for check points to monitor progress
FOCUS Instructional Priority Goals	SLT facilitating faculty meetings and working in grade-level/department groups	1. Analyze student data 2. Agree on instructional priorities 3. Identify instructional strategies 4. Determine professional development needs
PROCESS Action Planning Professional Development	SLT facilitating faculty meetings and working in grade-level/department groups	1. Finalize action plan and staff a faculty meeting for final agreement 2. Set up professional development schedule 3. Have SLT members support grade-level-teams in clarifying new instructional practices 4. Schedule checkpoints and benchmarks 5. Collect evidence to progress
OUTCOMES Monitor Progress and Report Results	SLT facilitating faculty meetings and working in grade-level/department groups	1. Assess and articulate results 2. Report results 3. Debrief lessons learned 4. Celebrate accomplishments 5. Identify next steps

development activities and other details of implementing the new instructional strategies that have been researched and selected by the grade-level teams.

The SLT uses the Checkpoint journal forms provided in the templates for the PLC school reform journal (see Figure 2.5) to capture reflections from the first of several checkpoints conducted by the SLT. It is important to monitor progress at scheduled checkpoints during the implementation

Figure 2.5   Checkpoint

Review your instructional priority goals

We met with our staff and reviewed the instructional priority goal of reading comprehension that was established at our last staff meeting. We also revisited the four phases of the action planning process—purpose, focus, process, and outcomes—to highlight that we were now moving into the process phase and that we would be building an action plan to implement our instructional priority schoolwide.

Build action plan

Our action plan included professional development in reading comprehension. Some of the professional development will be provided by staff members as part of our scheduled staff meetings, others will take place as part of our grade-level teams, and we are planning to attend a local professional development event where we hope to gain new understandings of "instructing" reading comprehension. Our principal has been very supportive with the additional resources we will need.

Clarify roles and responsibilities

Each grade-level team identified a lead, and each is going to clarify the reading comprehension strategy it will be using with its students. It is interesting to see how we are all interested and committed to impacting student performance in reading comprehension and the strategies vary from one grade level to another with some "strands" that are very similar, just developmentally adjusted for the student's readiness.

Establish professional development needs and plan

We want to have a shared understanding, as a staff, regarding reading comprehension, its relationship to other reading skills such as fluency and decoding and its unique cognitive abilities that we can learn to develop. Some staff members are researching—developing reading comprehension abilities—and plan to share their knowledge at our next scheduled checkpoint.

Set expected outcomes for instructional priority goals

As a staff, we are aiming to have a shared understanding of reading comprehension at our multigrade levels and for our students to accelerate their performance in reading and in their other subject areas. We are also focused on cross-curricular efforts to apply reading comprehension to all subject areas. We will use both standardized and formative assessment tools to determine progress.

process so that adaptations in the plan can be addressed based on progress data and other observations. Going to the fourth phase of the PLC school reform structured journal process, the SLT collects final data from the grade-level teams and schedules a final session with the faculty as represented on their So What? (Outcome) journal form (Figure 2.6).

Figure 2.6   So What? (Outcome)

RESULTS • REPORTING • CELEBRATION • NEXT STEPS

Share a summary evaluation of progress with priority goals

Because of our initial efforts to build a PLC in the form of a site leadership team focused on improving instruction, we have learned a great deal about teacher as leader and about the importance of collaborations and open communication among the staff.

As an SLT, we tried very hard to continually communicate and engage the entire staff in the process. We decided early to do everything we could to avoid the "in-group/ out-group" syndrome of having a team of peers appear to be in charge and "tell" others what to do. Over time, the staff seemed to gain respect for our efforts and appreciation for our commitment to engagement.

Each grade-level team provided their set of assessment data with comparisons to baseline assessment conducted in the fall. We then combined the results schoolwide and were able to "study" the impact of our efforts. All grade levels made progress and isolated the different strategies used at each grade level to assess the "powerful' strategies that seemed to have the greatest impact on student performance. In addition to published test, we did share observations and other artifacts regarding student observations and samples of student work.

Celebrate lessons learned and successes

We were eager to celebrate our success with student performance and especially our progress with a schoolwide instructional priority—something we had not attempted before. Most faculty members feel that we have establish a new level of collaboration among our staff and that in the future we can built on this platform of collaboration and relationship building to advance further with schoolwide instructional priorities.

Some staff members are more eager than others are to jump in again, and we are hoping the SLT structure will be sustained and that over time others will step up and become "teacher-leaders" as we take turn for service.

We are planning an extended celebration to include the parents and student who all contributed to our "push" on reading and reading comprehension in particular. All participants have a new level or understating of reading comprehension and an appreciation for each other's expertise and individual efforts that contributed to our "community" success.

SCHOOL REFORM WRAP-UP ■

Learning is the continual structuring and restructuring of ideas though interaction with people, objects, and ideas. (M G.. Brooks & J. Grennon-Brooks, 1999, p. 4)

Schoolwide reform efforts that have leadership sponsorship and the commitment of teacher leaders, serving as SLT members, are powerful structures and processes for improving instructional practices. The concept of SLTs and lateral leadership expands the scope of accountability for student outcomes on the entire staff as a PLC. The process, by design, gets the school reform effort into the classroom and influences the relationship between the teacher and students. This approach has brought school communities together, expanding their collective understanding about a shared purpose and a commitment to professional learning. Professional learning expands their repertoire and builds commitment to collegial collaborations for continuous improvements. Offering a process to clarify new understanding, take on new roles and shared responsibilities, and build a shared knowledge base related to professional practices can be accomplished when a PLC serving as an SLT in support of student achievement makes a commitment to using the structured journal process to guide and direct their process as they

1. establish a *purpose* for their SLT and engage the entire faculty;

2. identify instructional priorities as a *focus*;

3. design an action plan and implementation *process*;

4. move their plan into *action*;

5. reflect on the *outcome* and results of their effort;

6. celebrate results and identify next steps.

——HELPFUL HINTS——

When your SLT meets for the first time, set dates for scheduled staff meetings and checkpoints—to monitor progress. Make a commitment from the beginning, stick to the dates, and sustain engagement of the faculty. This will reinforce the shared responsibility of staff members and guard against staff members perceiving the SLT as an elite group—an in-group/out-group dynamic that could impact the collegial collaborations you are striving for to attain results.

3

Action Research Journal

Teacher as Researcher

The most superb effect of cooperative action research is synergy, in which products of collective thought and problem solving are greater than the sum of efforts of each individual working alone. (Schmuck, 1997, p. ix)

BACKGROUND OF ACTION RESEARCH ■

During the early decades of the twentieth century, educational philosopher John Dewey wrote about reflection and action as part of an educator's work. Since that time, many forms of research have developed in the teaching profession. As we enter the twenty-first century, the teacher as researcher, engaging in action research, holds great promise for creating learning communities.

For teacher-researchers in school settings today, questions of practice aimed at student achievement are the primary focus of action research. These questions can occur at the classroom level, or they can be drawn from dilemmas and reflections of thoughtful teachers on a daily basis.

Action research is a structured process for implementing new ideas to monitor progress and test the impact of new practices. Depending on the results, teachers make a decision to implement the new idea or to repeat the research cycle with adjustments in the practice to refine the innovation. It is a very basic systematic method to conduct research in the classroom:

1. Identify an inquiry, a banner question, based on observations and/ or data regarding student achievement.

2. Propose a solution and introduce a new practice or innovation and a plan to implement a new practice or intervention.

3. Implement the plan, with anticipated indicators of progress and a systematic process and timeline for progress monitoring.

4. Study the impact or outcome.

5. Determine next steps to implement the innovation or return the research process for further study and revise the solution.

For example, a group of teachers meet as a professional learning community (PLC), in their grade-level team. They have been looking at recent test scores in reading. Their main concern is that several fundamental skills such as decoding, sight vocabulary, and comprehension are below basic. As they take a closer look, they notice that even some students with higher overall language arts scores scored low in decoding. They decide to administer a formative assessment to determine a more detailed profile of student's strengths and weaknesses in decoding and to use that data as a baseline for instruction. They formed a workshop group to accelerate performance by building a foundational ability in decoding for identified students. Students participated in the decoding workshop for six weeks and their progress was monitored weekly. After the initial six weeks, the PLC looked at the progress data and determined that many of the students had improved in decoding and that in most instances their overall reading performance also had improved. Those who did not make progress with their overall reading performance will become part of the next iteration of the work of this PLC to accelerate student performance in reading.

Action research and inquiry conducted by a PLC can have a significant impact on teaching practices. This direct connection between inquiry and action is the power in the teacher as researcher. The people who *do* the work know best how to *improve* the work. When communities of professional educators come together to research their work, they are in the best position to make direct changes in their teaching practices.

Through action research teachers become confident about their work, more knowledgeable about school change, more likely to assume leadership roles, better able to communicate with colleagues, and more knowledgeable about the role of learning in teaching (Richert, 1994).

Many features of action research as a process underscore the role of learning. In the action research process, teachers examine questions that are important to them. As they draw from their experience and consider the questions that matter to them most, teachers become more aware of themselves as definers and constructors of knowledge and realize the power of their ideas. The structured journal process presented in this chapter serves as a guide to facilitate and coach action research as a professional tool for PLCs.

■ HOW TO USE THE ACTION RESEARCH JOURNAL

Clarifying the purpose of the PLC is first and foremost a useful strategy for the group members at the beginning is reviewing their norms and protocols, the processes for working together as a PLC. This will reaffirm what professional collaboration means to them and why they chose to use the structure and process of action research at this time. If you have not functioned as a PLC to this point, the group may use questions such as the following to orient members and establish ground rules:

- How have we previously worked together?
- Are we just getting to know each other?
- How would we like this group to function?

As the participants reflect, talk, and listen in an effort to establish a shared purpose and function for their learning community, they will naturally get acquainted and begin to build relationships.

Organization

PLCs are built on the capacity to collaborate and the commitment to listen, learn, and ask questions. A structured journal gives members of the group guidelines for initiating their action research by using the following goals or organizers:

1. **Establish a** *purpose*. Why are we forming our group? What is our overarching purpose and our desired outcome?

2. *Focus* **the inquiry.** What are the specific issues or dilemmas we hope to better understand?

3. **Design a** *process*. How will we pursue our inquiry? What activities will we engage in? What data will we collect? When will we meet to share findings and how will we collaborate? What are the time lines? What is our plan?

4. **Set an** *outcome*. How will we share our collection of data and our reflections to conclude and summarize our findings?

Action research supports teacher-researchers as they identify specific challenges within their classroom and research by planning, acting, reflecting, and revising. The four organizers of the journal process (purpose, focus, process, and outcome) contribute to a phase of the research process. Following is a model outline that reflects those organizers and shows the design of the structured journal as it applies to the action research process:

    I. Introduction

    II. Purpose

        A. Observations and data

    III. Focus

        A. Research target area

    IV. Process

        A. Plan

        B. Act (Implement)

        C. Refine (Monitor progress)

V. Outcome

   A. Reflections (Decisions regarding next steps)

Activities at each step guide the PLC in directing their action research inquiry as they collect data, observe learning, and refine practices.

Journal Design and Process

Purpose, focus, process, and outcome are key components in the action research journal process. The following is a model for the process denoting the actions and questions for reflection that characterize each component.

Why? (Purpose)

- How will our action research community impact student achievement?
- When will we meet to do this work?
- How will we make decisions to take action on outcomes?

What If? (Focus)

- What do we know about student performance?
- What are we especially interested in improving?
- What innovations and interventions might we consider?
- What are some of our concerns in our school community?

How Will It Work? (Process)

- When will we meet?
- How will we collect and analyze data?
- What process will we use for observations and monitoring progress/impact?
- How will we share roles and responsibilities in the group?

So What? (Outcome)

- How has our research impacted our work?
- How will we communicate findings?
- What actions will we take?

The action research journal process consists of the following actions as participants carry out the phases of purpose, focus, process, and outcome:

1. Participate in the initial purpose-setting process for action research.

2. Establish the target area for research.

3. Identify a collaboration network to support and enhance inquiry.

4. Collect information, strategies, skills, and materials related to the targeted research area.

5. Plan—design a plan to study target area.

6. Act—implement plan and assess impact.

7. Reflect and revise—engage in reflective collaborations and describe the outcome.

8. Consider making adaptations as indicated by research findings.

9. Assess the effectiveness of the action research process.

The action research journal can serve as a tool to focus and direct conversations and research activities as well as to assist with drawing conclusions about research findings. The process can bring participants together around a common purpose such as how to deal with a key decision or with a dilemma the school is facing. When working with a group of educators and other learning community members, a facilitator can assess their readiness regarding collaboration by asking questions such as the following:

- Have we worked together before?
- Are we an established PLC?
- Do we have norms and protocols for working together?

If the participants lack a shared history of working together in a collaborative way, the facilitator might want to begin with activities and discussions for establishing a PLC. The initial focus might be on building a community (shared understanding and beliefs). These preliminary conversations will build a foundation for the group to clarify their purpose and desired outcome in terms of the action research process.

CASE STUDY: ACTION RESEARCH JOURNAL ■

Following is an overview of the journaling process, including samples of journals and activities from actual action research experiences within a school community. On the journal pages in this section, participants' responses are set in italics so that the various types of notes and reflections that are prompted by the journaling process can be easily identified. Commentary is provided before each form explaining how the group under study applied the journaling process to facilitate action research as a framework for school change.

When you, as a facilitator or member of a learning community, are ready to apply the journaling process, note that the journal templates for action research shown here are offered at the end of this at the end of this book on page 89 and on the accompanying CD.

The questions at the top of the first journal template, Figure 3.1, address the purpose of and serve as organizers for discussions about why the group is forming, what the participants' beliefs and concerns are, and how the group will schedule meetings.

At this point, the group participants orient themselves to the action research journal design and begin the first step of the process: establishing purpose.

Figure 3.1 Why? (Purpose)

OBSERVATIONS • CONCERNS • QUESTIONS

- How will our action research community impact student achievement?

- When will we meet to do this work?

- How will we make decisions to take action on outcomes?

The action research journal provides a framework for identifying, planning, and facilitating research. It provides opportunities for

1. identifying a target area for research;

2. building a research plan;

3. collecting information;

4. collaborating with peers as research partners;

5. observing;

6. assessing impact of strategies used in target area;

7. refining practices; and

8. reflecting on experiences.

Purpose Statement

The purpose of our action research team is to determine the impact of class size on student learning. Now that we have reduced our first-grade classes to twenty students (previously thirty-three students), we anticipate greater opportunities for individualized instruction and that student learning will improve. We hope to prove the impact on student learning and to document the shift in our instructional practices.

Using an observation template (see Figure 3.2), group participants reflect on their observations about current practices and student learning.

The next step of the journaling process is focus—identifying a specific area for action research and inquiry (see Figure 3.3). The group participants reflect on the banner questions, the key questions that will drive their inquiry and work. The banner questions are used to facilitate discussion and identify the target for research.

The participants use the Research Target template (see Figure 3.4) to guide discussions. Lead-ins or sentence stems are instrumental to reflection in the action research journal process.

Having determined the research target, the participants move to the process step of the journal. Using the questions in the Process template (see Figure 3.5), the participants determine their plan, their method(s) of data collection, and their methods of collaboration. A facilitator may use the Guide for Professional Collaboration and A Guide for Listening templates in the Guides and Resources section at the back of the book and on the accompanying CD.

Figure 3.2   Observations

1. What are your observations regarding student learning?

    Since we have lowered the class size, I am noticing subtle differences in how some students listen, follow directions, and are aware of communication in the classroom. I am able to move the class through activities in less time and it seems to take less practice for them to establish routines in class.

2. Describe strategies and practices that have been effective and others that have not worked so well.

    I have been trying to decide on an effective way to implement learning centers. One of our goals in the class-size reduction process is to schedule more individualized instructional time and to apply a diagnostic teaching model. I have been trying to identify appropriate independent tasks for students to do at the centers.

3. What are your interests and concerns about your work?

    I realize there is a need to document student learning and to provide data and dialogues that reflect improvement in student learning. My greatest concern is that we might be asking for results that are developmentally inappropriate. I am concerned that we might begin to establish inappropriate expectations of young students.

Figure 3.3   What If? (Focus)

Banner Questions

- What do we know about student performance?

- What are we especially interested in improving?

- What innovations and interventions might we consider?

- What are some of our concerns in our school community?

Research Team Establishes a Research Target

We as researchers reflect on observations and learnings from teaching experiences and pose questions. These questions represent puzzling experiences such as, "How can I determine readiness to begin reading with such diversity among my first-grade class?" These observations and questions will help us build a pathway for identifying strategies and employing innovative practices to research and study the connections among theories, practice, and students' learning.

Research Focus Discussion

Our group has brainstormed all of our concerns and interests regarding class size reduction and how to best focus our research. We have decided to focus on the development of literacy abilities. We will collect data that will help us trace student development and learning in the area of literacy and reading in particular.

Figure 3.4   Research Target

What is the impact of class size reduction on student learning in the area of literacy development and reading in particular?

1. Action Questions

    What if…

    we all used the same inventory materials to assess student growth?

    How about…

    working together to align our instructional materials and practices in the first-grade classrooms?

    How could I…

    document and reflect on my observations and changes in my practices as a result of smaller class size?

2. Collegial Connections

    What practices and models have others used? Are my colleagues having similar experiences?

3. Strategies and Skills to Implement

    Our goal is…

    to complete a literacy system within our school.

    We need to address…

    how we will select assessment materials to document growth. How the system will work. How we will work together to standardize the assessment process among our first-grade team members.

Figure 3.5   How Will It Work? (Process)

PLAN • DATA COLLECTION • COLLABORATION

-   When will we meet?
-   How will we collect data?
-   What process will we use for observations and information gathering?
-   How will we share roles and responsibilities in the group?

Research Plan

-   Strategies to be employed
-   Implementation plan
-   Data collection template
-   Observations and reflective collaborations
-   Refinements of the plan

Next, using the Research Plan Strategy template (Figure 3.6), partici-pants determine their plan of action, the preparation needed, and the schedule for implementation.

The challenge in the process is to use the structured journal effectively to organize and guide a plan and strategy for research. If the participants have clearly agreed on a purpose and have identified a research target, they should be able to generate action questions that focus specifically on what they—as a learning community—want to learn from the actions they take and the data they collect.

Using the Data Collection template (Figure 3.7), the group—having established what data they need to collect—endeavors to keep the data collection system as simple as possible. As teacher-researchers, group par-ticipants realize that data collection is a critical step in the action research process.

Figure 3.6   Research Plan Strategy Form

We will meet as a grade level once every two weeks to share findings and observations, and to refine process. We will begin with identifying critical literacy areas to assess first graders to establish a baseline for study. Where are the students in terms of their development and abilities? We will assess letter recognition, sound/symbol relationship (long and short vowels), word recognition, fluency, and listening comprehension.

Preparation

Materials: _What assessment materials will we use?_

Methods: _How will we practice and observe the assessment process with each other? How will we collect data?_

Resources: _What will our needs be in terms of materials and release time? What is available to us? In what areas would we like staff development?_

Implementation Schedule

August _Area meeting—establish purpose and action targets._

September _Discuss developmental literacy. Assessment planning for literacy._

October _Begin baseline data collection._

November _Share assessment findings and study literacy profiles of students._

December _Explore literacy staff development that aligns with students' needs from assessments._

January _Plan for midyear assessments._

February _Discuss staff developments and practices used by team members: what is working and what we want to know more about._

March _Collect data from fall and midyear assessments and reflect on findings; discuss connections to staff development design._

May _Collect final assessment data._

June _Draw conclusions from student growth patterns and instructional practices. Make recommendations for continued study next term._

It is important to remember that *what* data are collected and *how* the data are collected will determine the validity of the action research, particularly when conclusions are drawn. The data collection system in the action research process should not be so complex that it interferes with regular routines or makes the data less meaningful.

The final session for the group is devoted to the outcome step of the process (see Figure 3.8). Each group participant draws conclusions, speaks as an individual and as a group member, and makes suggestions for change based on the group's action research.

To close the action research journal process, the group celebrates their accomplishments as a learning community and considers identifying steps for further inquiry. A facilitator may use the Thoughtful Questions for Learning Communities template in the Guides and Resources section at the back of the book and on the accompanying CD.

Figure 3.7   Data Collection Form

Collecting and Analyzing Multiple Sources of Data to Study the Impact of Action Plans

WHO (demographic data to be collected)

Number of Students:

Gender: M _____ F _____

Stable student population (over three years):

Attendance:

Other:

HOW (processing of data and strategies in research plan)

Focusing on events that are happening and things we are doing related to our target action area. For example, collect numbers to chart frequency and seek patterns. Since the target area is writing and we are trying new writing strategies, collect some of the following data:

> *Students are writing (x) times a week.*

> *We are meeting in writing groups (x) times monthly.*

SO WHAT (outcomes—formal and informal data)

Assessment

> *Formal and/or traditional testing*

> *Alternative assessment*

> *Feedback and observations*

Other Outcomes

> *Impacts expected and unexpected from action plan*

Surveys

> *Comments from students*

Figure 3.8   So What? (Outcome)

CONCLUSIONS • REFLECTIONS • REFINEMENTS • LEARNINGS

Because of working in our action research team, I realized the power of collaboration and how much I was able to learn from my colleagues. We have been doing a lot of the same things and experiencing many similar problems, and yet we never had an opportunity to discuss them.

We have just begun to clarify our purpose for the long term. Probably we had very high expectations for ourselves when we began, trying to do too much in one year. We did learn that the diagnostic model is very helpful for understanding children's development of literacy abilities. Continuing our conversation about what is a balanced, individualized literacy staff development will be very important.

Has the class size reduction made a difference with student learning? Yes! We have been better able to focus on multiple aspects of the developing literacy process and to customize, assess, and support the development process. Next year, if we continue to collect and share data for each of our students, I am sure we will see the overall differences with end of the term achievement levels as compared to the number of students with delayed learning problems entering second grade in the past.

I observed the effectiveness of learning centers in my class with smaller class size. I was better able to identify students' independent levels for working at the centers and to prepare students for participating in the routine of "center time." There was virtually no wasted time addressing problems at the centers while I was conducting individual reading conferences.

What hypotheses did you bring to your research target area?

I thought class size reduction would make my job easier; I also thought that students would learn at a faster rate with individual attention. Both of these seemed to be validated by our data collections and collegial sharing.

How did the data collection support your learning?

The data collection helped me target key areas of literacy development and have specific information to customize a literacy staff development for each student. The data collection also helped in our discussions about the most effective practices and materials.

What new questions have emerged from your research?

I would like to continue to study, along with my group, the long-term impact of class size reduction and of how we can better capitalize on our use of time and resources. I would like to address how we can share data with parents and gain confidence in the community support for smaller class size.

■ ACTION RESEARCH WRAP-UP

Action research is a powerful process for focusing on inquiry and data collection. As revealed in the previous case study, working as an individual as well as with colleagues—as part of a learning community—is key to the process.

Selecting a research target area that is integral to your professional work has everything to do with a successful action research journal experience. That way, your work as a teacher-researcher will not be considered an add-on to your regularly scheduled duties.

As part of a learning community, you will have a process for reflecting, collaborating, and learning from your daily interactions in class. Because of action research, you and your group will have new information to *inform* and *improve* teaching practices throughout the school community as you work meaningfully toward school change.

Using the structured journal as a guide, you

1. establish a *purpose* for your research;

2. identify a *focus*, a research target;

3. design a *plan* and *process* for research;

4. move your plan into *action*;

5. reflect on the *outcome*;

6. *revise* practices and work toward change, as indicated by research.

——HELPFUL HINTS——

Having a container for your research data and notes—your collection of artifacts, evidence, and so on—is always helpful. Consider a zipper bag, a roomy canvas bag, or a file box filled with folders.

District Portfolio of Schools

Constructing a School Portfolio

Community building must become the heart of any school improvement effort…it requires us to think community, believe in community, and practice community. (Sergiovanni, 1994, p. xi)

BACKGROUND OF THE SCHOOL PORTFOLIO ■

When a school community engages in the process of constructing their school portfolio, they must take a keen look at their values, priorities, and commitment to supporting achievement for all students who enter their school. This is an important step toward a school district building a system of schools aimed at accelerating student achievement. In these times of annual yearly progress (AYP), program improvement, and the need for districts to offer options to students and parents in selecting an alternative school within their district, a portfolio of schools becomes more than a mix of schools among which students choose. It is a strategy for creating an entire system that sets high standards for key elements in a high-performing school and invites each school to engage in the process as an opportunity for district change. The school portfolio can be used for a variety of purposes, such as to

- present the values and commitments and key elements that are indicators of the quality instruction and results;
- offer options to students in selecting a school placement that is most aligned with a student's academic needs;

- report on the status of school programs and student progress to the community at large; and
- celebrate accomplishments and plan for the future.

The portfolio can also be used as part of the process that schools go through as they apply for educational grants.

As presented in this chapter, the school portfolio, facilitated by using a structured journal process, provides a framework for professional learning community (PLC) members to demonstrate accomplishments and establish priorities for the school and school district.

The Role of Portfolios in No Child Left Behind

The school portfolio has the flexibility to be a useful tool in a variety of areas. In addition to those listed previously, the portfolio process supports several essential areas of the No Child Left Behind (NCLB) initiative.

Evidence-Based Practices

NCLB calls for annual statewide testing to monitor student progress toward standards. It also calls for evidence-based practices that will yield products of student progress.

- The portfolio can assist with tracking progress during the school year by organizing evidences of student learning. Collecting multiple sources of student data such as student work and classroom assessments provides products of student progress at various checkpoints.

Parental Involvement

NCLB encourages choices for parents regarding the schooling environment for their child.

- The portfolio provides a container and a process for parents, students, and teachers to review evidences of student learning and agree to program adjustment when indicated. It offers parents an opportunity to be involved with their child's learning as a partner in monitoring progress and understanding targeted state standards.

Customized Learning for Individual Students

NCLB often requires individualized learning plans with customized, differentiated instruction that assures each child has the opportunity to achieve in school.

- The portfolio provides a record and a process for organizing a child's learning profile and aligning his or her unique learning needs to a customized program for meeting the standards.

Looking at Student Work

NCLB stresses teacher competency and supports ongoing professional learning for teachers.

- The portfolio offers an opportunity for collegial coaching and job embedded learning. Teachers can use the portfolio as a framework for collegial conversations. Through these protocol conversations, teachers expand and deepen their understandings. Using professional development resources, teachers have opportunities to learn about additional research-based practices for improving achievement and enhancing each child's learning.

HOW TO USE THE SCHOOL PORTFOLIO JOURNAL   ■

Many districts and school communities have established PLCs at grade levels, for departments, and as a site leadership team. These professional structures have been transformed into PLCs by establishing their norms and protocols for professional practices and clarifying their primary purpose and commitments to their professional work. If your school community has established a PLC, the school portfolio process will surely be enhanced by their facilitation of the process.

Organization

Like the other frameworks presented in this book, the school portfolio is organized around four phases (purpose, focus, process, and outcome). As envisioned in the case study in this chapter, those involved in the school portfolio process often devote a session or meeting to each phase. Activities at each phase guide the participants in focusing and directing their efforts. After collecting artifacts and evidence to demonstrate learnings and establish plans for school programs and classroom practices, participants share their observations, reflections, and priorities as part of the process. The portfolio process, facilitated by journaling, culminates in a final product: the school portfolio.

Journal Process and Design

The school portfolio journal is a process designed as a tool for the PLC to facilitate the school community as they articulate, demonstrate, and illustrate their purpose, programs, and progress. Following is a template for using the journaling process including actions that characterize the four phases.

Why? (Purpose)

- Is it for planning for school improvement or implementing a new program?
- Is it for organizing for an educational grant application?
- Is it for telling the story of the school's journey and accomplishments for the year?

What If? (Focus)

- Define the programs and/or priorities that school community members have identified as the subject for the portfolio.
- Involve the learning community in the school portfolio (which often includes teachers, parents, administrators, community leaders, local business people, and consultants) to work together in identifying all the parts of the total program.
- If the structured journal process is being used to demonstrate school community accomplishments, the portfolio group might focus on those aspects of the school program that contributed to those successes.
- If the process is being used to assess the current status of the school and to develop a plan for change, the group may identify priorities by using a graphic organizer—such as the Action Priority Wheel presented in this chapter's case study.

How Will It Work? (Process)

Construct the school portfolio. If multiple priorities or programs have been identified, participants can break themselves down into small groups and devote themselves to a particular priority or program. Using the structured journal to facilitate the process, the small group members may ask the following questions:

- What is the purpose of the program or priority?
- What specific area of schooling does it focus on?
- How will the process work?
- How will the program or priority be integrated with the whole school portfolio?
- What will be the outcome (the accomplishments)?

When each small group has gone through this process, all the participants can reconvene in a portfolio working session, at which time learnings and plans for the portfolio can be shared with the whole learning community.

So What? (Outcome)

- Review the school portfolio process and final product.
- Determine future goals and actions for the school community in general.

■ CASE STUDY: SCHOOL PORTFOLIO JOURNAL

Following is an overview of the structured journal process including samples of journals and activities from actual school portfolio experiences. On the journal pages in this section, participants' responses are set in italics so that the various types of notes and reflections that are prompted by the process can be easily identified. Commentary is provided before each form explaining how the group optimized the structured journal process to the school portfolio.

When you, a facilitator or learning community member, are ready to apply the structured journal process with your colleagues, note that journal templates for the school portfolio shown here are offered at the end of this chapter and on the accompanying CD.

To begin the school portfolio process, the group in this case study designs a cover for their portfolio—much like a masthead of a publication (see Figure 4.1).

In the school portfolio process, all members of the community should have an opportunity to participate, as they wish. The PLC, acting as the lead facilitator, in this particular case study have invited parents, teachers, and administrators, as well as other school staff and local business people who are in partnership with the school, to join in the process of articulating priorities and accomplishments.

Agreement regarding purpose, or defining their shared purpose and desired outcome, is a critical starting point. It builds the foundation for effective design and process of the portfolio. The portfolio can best serve as a connection between the institution and the individual when a joint purpose is clearly agreed upon from the start.

Using the Guide for Defining Purpose (Figure 4.2) to coach the process, the group begins to determine the purpose of the school portfolio.

Figure 4.1   Portfolio

School Name

Monroe Avenue Elementary School

School Portfolio Team Facilitator

Helen Campbell, Principal

Names of Team Members

_____

_____

_____

_____

_____

_____

Figure 4.2   Guide for Defining Purpose

The school portfolio is an organizer for planning and reflecting on continuous school improvement. It is a framework for working together to identify school priorities and to exhibit student learning outcomes.

The school portfolio process provides a structure for

- facilitating change;
- working together as a staff and school community;
- organizing, planning, and assessing student outcomes;
- collecting artifacts and evidences;
- building community relationships;
- reflecting on values and attitudes;
- drawing on past experiences and knowledge;
- exploring possibilities;
- building new understandings about priorities.

To work toward defining a purpose, the school portfolio team members will

1. consider their definition of common purpose and formulate and share their philosophy, highlighting belief systems about the purpose and process of education;

2. learn about the portfolio process as a tool for organizing school planning;

3. build communication abilities and listening skills.

Next, the team members move toward consensus in the purpose step as they go through the structured process. The portfolio team has

- clarified the context for decision making with school administration;
- determined a standard or rubric for their work;
- set parameters for their collaboration.

At this point, team members go to the Why? (Purpose) journal template (Figure 4.3), reflecting personally on the role of schooling in their community as part of the school portfolio process. A facilitator may also use the Worksheet for Defining Purpose and Priorities, School Portfolio Survey, and A Strategy for Determining Top Priorities for School Change templates in the Guides and Resources section at the back of the book and on the accompanying CD.

Figure 4.3   Why? (Purpose)

OBSERVATIONS • CONCERNS • QUESTIONS

1.   **From my perspective, the primary indicators of student learning are…**

when students are asking questions, engaged with a high level of energy in their school work, and making steady progress academically. Their actual written work is a product, but not always the only or best indicator that they, in fact, are learning. I think we need to observe our students and ask them questions in order to be assured learning is taking place.

2.   **My personal theory about how students learn is…**

kids learn from doing and from having someone guide them as they practice new skills. They learn when they are in a risk-free environment in which they are not afraid to try and try again. Not all kids learn the same way: some learn by talking, and others by doing. Others learn by watching and listening. We need to accommodate a variety of learning styles and student needs.

3.   **At our school, I am most proud of…**

the way we all work together as a school community. Even though we do not always agree on an issue, we are willing to talk about it. An outstanding accomplishment is our student-run school store, which provides products that display school spirit and teaches students real-world business skills.

Moving on to the focus phase, the school portfolio team uses the journaling process to focus their work by establishing priorities, or entry points, to demonstrate and exhibit current achievements within the school portfolio framework. Using the What If? (Focus) form (Figure 4.4) to coach the process, they discuss and reflect on needs and goals for continuous school improvement.

During the focus phase of the school portfolio process, the team members collaborate and design structures to work together in priority action

Figure 4.4   What If? (Focus)

At the focus phase of the process, the school portfolio team will

1.   define the priorities for the school community;

2.   select the top six or eight priorities using the Action Priority Wheel (Figure 4.5);

3.   form priority work groups accordingly.

Ideally, each priority work group is a mixture of parents, teachers, and other school community members. The teachers can check in with colleagues regarding the collections of artifacts and program descriptions. The parents and other members can enhance the process with their various perspectives. The process of conversations and collaborations within these groups builds school community.

Figure 4.5 Action Priority Wheel

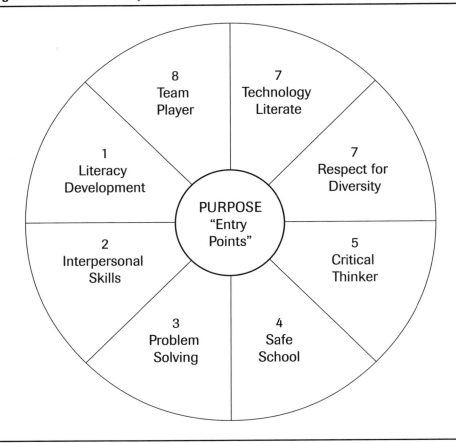

teams. The team uses the Action Priority Wheel exercise (Figure 4.5) to facilitate this process as they engage in the following steps:

1. Brainstorm all ideas, suggestions, needs, and wants.

2. Break into small groups and combine similar ideas, forming a list of priorities within these small groups.

3. Reconvene and share the small group priority lists; compile a master priority list that represents priorities for all participating community members.

4. Post the priority list at the front of the room.

5. Cast votes for priorities by using peel-and-stick colored dots—or by making slash marks with a marker pen—on the chart paper next to their priority(s) of choice. (Each team member is allowed three votes. The team members are aware they may use all three votes for one priority or divide their votes in any manner they wish.)

6. Place the top six or eight priorities in the Action Priority Wheel. The wheel image illustrates or implies that all priorities are important and interdependent. (A member may select *explore student outcomes* as his or her priority, yet he or she is well aware that all aspects of the learning process contribute to student outcomes.)

7. Work in the priority action groups of choice based on the voting process. Members use the prompts on the Action Priority Wheel to guide their group sessions as they clarify the current and future efforts in their priority area by discussing how they will represent purpose and progress.

Addressing what artifacts to include in the school portfolio that will represent their accomplishments and commitment, the members reflect on how they are currently supporting and achieving their priority. Group members include a discussion of future plans in their priority area.

At this point, the school portfolio team in this case study have several types of three-ring binders or containers handy, so they are prepared to organize and display the various artifacts (evidence such as a student achievement chart) that will tell the story about the priorities and accomplishments of the school. As the team members enter this phase of the process, they are prepared to use the same presentation format to introduce their priorities and to describe current and future efforts. The various groups exhibit their artifacts and evidence to illustrate their desired outcomes. Ideally, when these individual priority groups combine their work, the end product (the school portfolio) has continuity in terms of design.

Using the How Will It Work? (Process) template (Figure 4.6) as a facilitation tool, the team moves on to the third step of the school portfolio process. A facilitator uses the Student Profile Checklist (see the template found in the Guides and Resources section at the back of the book and on the accompanying CD) to identify student outcomes as part of the collaboration process determining a shared purpose and priorities for the school portfolio.

Each priority action team uses the Priority Action Team Worksheet (Figure 4.7) to prompt reflection on the focus of their work together. For purposes of this case study, one priority action team has chosen *literacy development* as the priority on which to focus.

Figure 4.6   How Will It Work? (Process)

PLAN • DATA COLLECTION • COLLABORATION

At the process phase, the team will

1. agree on a design and format for the school portfolio;

2. meet with community members in their individual priority action teams;

3. identify existing and future programs and practices that contribute to the various priorities;

4. consider future programs and practices to support priorities for change;

5. describe impact of existing programs;

6. collect artifacts and evidences of accomplishments;

7. agree on a plan for checkpoints (meetings to ascertain progress), as well as a time line for completion of the school portfolio.

Figure 4.7   Priority Action Team Worksheet

Priority Description

Our school priority is literacy development. We feel literacy (listening, speaking, reading, and writing) is the key to school success and learning.

Current Accomplishments

We have literacy portfolios, collections of various students' writings and reflections (journaling) about favorite stories they have read. The portfolios also contain a book actually written and bound by the students.

We have published authors visit our school two times a year to speak with the students about becoming a writer and the importance of dedication to writing and reading books.

We have established a Parents-and-Reading Club that meets with the reading specialist once a month. At these meetings, parents learn about the reading and writing process, about how their students are being instructed, and about how they can support the learning process at home. There is always time for discussing special interests and concerns expressed by parents, which often assists in planning a topic for the next session.

In literacy portfolio sharing, students visit other classrooms every Friday to share individual portfolios with a partner. Each partner writes notes in the visitor's portfolio registry, commenting on the portfolio, recording the event with the date, and signing his or her name.

Future Plans and Suggestions

In the future, we plan to have Family Library Night when family members accompany students for an evening at the school library, expressly for selecting and reading books together. We are also in the process of designing a process for individualized literacy plans for each student. These plans will be customized to meet students' various developing needs in each area of the reading process.

Senior citizens will be visiting our classes to read to students and to contribute to their reading logs on a regular basis.

At this point, priority team members consult with others for information and bring program descriptions from their various classrooms or school sites as well as seek ideas for future plans to bring to the next scheduled checkpoint meeting. At checkpoint meetings during the focus phase, the small group members

- share programs and descriptions;
- use a journaling form that is appropriate for the agreed-upon school portfolio format;
- share artifacts and select the most appropriate ones for programs and special event descriptions;
- write descriptions of artifacts for the school portfolio;
- reaffirm next checkpoint meeting date, making sure the priority team is on schedule with the agreed-upon time line for the school portfolio team as a whole.

Figure 4.8   Artifacts and Evidence Registry

Briefly list here any artifacts and evidence that represent actions for the selected priority.

Priority: *Literacy Instruction*

> *Samples of student writing portfolios*
>
> *Assessments and individualized literacy plans*
>
> *Videotape of student reading*
>
> *Class stories generated by students*
>
> *Copies of registries from various students' literacy portfolios, showing dates and visitors*

Each priority action group completes the Artifacts and Evidence Registry (Figure 4.8) to facilitate the record keeping that is essential for this step of the process. Eventually, the school portfolio team compiles the registries in a binder as part of the school portfolio.

As the team members compile the school portfolio for display, they include action team priority information along with a portfolio purpose statement at the beginning. They have a section in the school portfolio devoted to each priority. The priorities will vary from school to school, which is what makes the portfolio, a product constructed by a team for that particular school community, an authentic process.

As the team proceeds to the fourth and last phase of the process, they use the So What? (Outcome) journal template (Figure 4.9) to reflect on the ultimate goals and accomplishments of the school portfolio and learnings from the process.

Figure 4.9   So What? (Outcome)

CONCLUSIONS • REFLECTIONS • REFINEMENTS • LEARNINGS

1. Prepare the final product (the school portfolio) to be displayed at the school site.

2. Each priority team will contribute descriptions of programs and practices as well as the purpose for each priority section in the school portfolio binder. Members will also include artifacts and evidence of priorities and future plans.

3. The portfolio will be exhibited to the entire school community and will continue to serve as a presentation or album portfolio for orienting new families to the school.

4. Each year the portfolio can be revisited and updates can be added to reflect the process of continual school improvement.

■ SCHOOL PORTFOLIO WRAP-UP

Constructing a school portfolio is an opportunity for members of the school community to come together and discuss their priorities and progress in achieving their outcomes for student learning. The school leadership team, the parent organization, and site administrator(s) all have an opportunity to participate on the school portfolio team, as well as to collect, reflect, and select artifacts and evidence of student successes to feature in the school portfolio.

The school portfolio journal can assist portfolio team members in collecting artifacts for their portfolio as they reaffirm their shared purpose, priorities, and outcomes for students in the community. When the portfolio is completed, it can serve as a hallmark album to be shared with others, a process that describes and illustrates the priorities, achievements, and future plans for the school.

Using the structured journal as a guide, the school portfolio process is easy to follow as you

- begin with developing a shared *purpose;*
- determine a *focus* or action priorities;
- establish a *process* for collecting artifacts (evidence) that describe strategies and outcomes for action priorities and represent a design for the portfolio;
- exhibit the *outcome* and share the portfolio as an album of achievements and plans for the future of the school community.

——HELPFUL HINTS——

As recommended, decide ahead of time—as a team—what form and design you want for the school portfolio, so that when each priority group comes together to compile the school portfolio, it flows like a storybook.

5

Professional Performance Journal

The Highly Qualified Teacher

Continuous development of all teachers is the cornerstone for meaning, improvement and reform. Professional development and school development are intrinsically linked. (Fullan, 1991, p. 315)

BACKGROUND OF PROFESSIONAL GROWTH AND PERFORMANCE

Professional development and performance—specifically in terms of the portfolio—is a process that supports teacher learning and contributes to establishing new norms for professional development and evaluation. Portfolios began to emerge as a valuable tool for focusing, organizing, and facilitating professional learning as early as the 1980s. In the Professional Development Consortium's pilot project in the late 1980s, teachers successfully used the learner portfolio framework, a portfolio structure, and process that was not only teacher directed and supported by peer collaboration, but also endorsed by the school administration.

A history of the development of the professional portfolio has to include the benchmark work reported by Wolf in a 1991 *Kappan* article. The subject of the article was using the portfolio as a collection of items such as a presentation portfolio for exhibiting and/or recording professional accomplishments of teachers with a focus on the TAP, the Teacher

Assessment Project at Stanford done in collaboration with Lee Schulman (Wolf, 1991).

Wolf (1991) reported that, while the TAP project was intended to assist with the design and plans for the National Board of Teaching Standards, it ultimately led to the notion of the *working portfolio* as teacher evaluation. The portfolio approach envisioned by the TAP project was one in which others direct the nature of and the process by which the artifacts and evidence are collected and exhibited by the learner (the teacher).

In February 1989, however, Christopher Clark of Michigan State University introduced a completely different course of action as he presented a paper on professional growth at the International Conference on Teacher Development. In his presentation, he described *self-directed* professional development of teachers—an approach quite different from the "evaluation by others" approach exemplified by the TAP project. Clark's plan did not mention using a portfolio, but it did recommend a design for teachers to self-assess and reflect on their practices. Addressing an important turning point for professional growth, Clark analyzed the research on "teacher thinking" and the teacher as learner approach (reflection and collaboration as opposed to evaluation by others), a movement that had begun back in 1976.

Today this framework of professional growth is viewed as a valuable tool and as a structure to focus and facilitate growth in professional practices. The focus for learning, the *essential question* for inquiry, is learner generated and aimed at connecting identified student needs and instructional priorities with teacher's learning. As I first envisioned it in a 1989 study (Dietz, 1993), the educator's professional portfolio is designed today around the same four steps seen throughout this book:

- **Purpose.** Asking why you are using a professional development portfolio
- **Focus.** Asking what is our theme or focus for professional learning
- **Process.** Asking how will we collaborate as a PLC to learn, practice, and reflect
- **Outcome.** Asking how will we know it is working and what we want to learn next

This portfolio process, specifically tailored to the professional portfolio as a framework for professional learning communities (PLCs), has led to revising the collaboration and evaluation process for educators nationwide. After its introduction to the public schools in Orange County, Florida, in 1994, the professional portfolio process outlined in this chapter was adopted countywide as part of the teacher assessment system. The New York City Teacher Center Consortium completed their pilot study on the professional portfolio in 1995; currently, the portfolio is an alternative assessment option for teachers in the New York City public schools. PLCs acting as site leadership teams (SLTs) are using this structure and process for accountability and assessment of the work of SLTs as they construct their campus improvement plans aimed at student achievement. The professional portfolio process continues to be adapted for emerging needs. Since 2006, several districts in California, Texas, and New York have used the portfolio process to focus their work and monitor results in these times of high stakes accountability.

Often, professional portfolios are viewed—at least initially—as a collection of items to be reviewed and, in some cases, evaluated by another individual without the learner (the creator of the portfolio) being present. However, the portfolio concept as presented in this text is more about the professional portfolio as an organizer or process for deepening the levels of understandings, exploration, and assimilation of new thinking about teaching and learning practices. As such, the portfolio is not created or evaluated in isolation, it is not measured by a simple rubric, and since it is a process rather than a collection of items, it is not viewed as being consumable.

Portfolios that have gone in that single dimension, as a collection rather than a process, have lost the dynamics of inquiry, collaboration, and reflection for learning. This is a significant loss since the mission of teachers today is to become self-directed and assert leadership actions. Journaling as part of the portfolio process offers role flexibility, dialogue, reflection, conversation, and collaboration, which allow educators to fulfill their mission in terms of professional growth. The portfolio process is reciprocal, not hierarchical, inviting uncertainty as well as thoughtful reconsideration and restructuring.

Many school districts across the nation have made the commitment to use PLCs as a venue for teacher collaboration and learning and have successfully used the portfolio as a means of focusing and facilitating professional growth.

Many positive results have occurred because of offering the professional portfolio as a learning opportunity (an opportunity for professional growth) to teachers. In the early 1990s, Graves (1996) at the University of Ohio, Dayton, conducted a four-year case study on the implementation of the portfolio process in schools and reported the following findings:

- Teachers found the professional development portfolio to be an excellent framework to gain focus on their personal and professional growth.
- Portfolio development stages were different for each participant.
- Once it was established that teachers would have control over their own professional growth, they needed time to adjust to the change.
- After having engaged in the professional portfolio process, teachers no longer felt the need to refer to a prescribed organization; they had internalized the process.
- Learning to self-assess involved time, feedback, and reflection on the part of teachers.

These benefits and changes represent an important opportunity for educators to take charge of their professional development and learning.

Portfolios: A Response for Highly Qualified Educators

No Child Left Behind (NCLB) has had a significant impact on how we do our work. It brings the best of intentions for *closing the achievement gap* and has challenged educators to assess how they use their time and resources to create and sustain efficient and effective systems—a system that is learner focused and results oriented. High on the list of learners are administrators and teachers, the professionals who inform and implement reform efforts to accelerate student achievement.

NCLB Requirements for Teachers

One key goal of the federal reauthorization of the Elementary and Secondary Education Act (ESEA), also known as the NCLB Act of 2001, is that *all* students are taught by highly qualified teachers. To this end, each local educational agency (LEA) must develop a plan to ensure that all elementary, middle, and high school teachers who are assigned to teach core academic subjects meet the NCLB requirements to ensure they are highly qualified.

To implement these teacher requirements, changes are necessary to align current statewide credentialing and professional development practices with NCLB goals. The portfolio process provides a structure for aligning performance requirements with professional learning opportunities and supports a job-embedded professional development model.

The portfolio process is designed using a systems model and is organized around four dynamic phases for a comprehensive learning process. The following section gives an example of how the portfolio supports job-embedded learning by aligning with key requirements and the essential design elements of the portfolio process to optimize the time and potential for teacher as learner.

Performance Portfolio Journal

- **Purpose.** To clarify professional goals and key requirements to qualifying for an identified professional placement such as elementary teacher, special education teacher, or reading specialist
- **Focus.** To concentrate on goals and essential questions aligned to the key assessments and learnings to meet requirements as a highly qualified teacher
- **Process.** To plan, set goals, collect evidence of learning, and meet key requirements including professional development activities, state testing programs, and coaching/mentoring conversations regarding the program and plan to attain key requirements to be highly qualified teacher in your chosen professional area of work
- **Outcomes.** To demonstrate performance results

Most performance assessments for teachers are based on local and/or state standards for the teaching profession and are tied to accelerating student achievement, which are central to school improvement and expectations in NCLB. These standards articulate what teachers should know and be able to do to improve schools and increase student learning while supporting the accountability requirements for school improvement and student achievement.

There is a collection of standards for the teaching profession, the National Board of Teaching Standards, as well as state-by-state sets of teaching standards for teachers. These standards have been used for evaluation, credentialing, and professional development planning. Among them are emerging key themes and attributes of professional teaching standards:

1. Collaborations with colleagues to improve professional repertoire for student centered instruction.

2. Establish and sustain an efficient, safe, and effective classroom environment to support and promote student engagement and learning.

3. Engage with parents and school community members to support student learning and optimizing resources and expertise.

4. Establish and maintain understanding of research-based practices and on going collaboration with colleagues in your area of practice. Sustain focus in your area of expertise such as your specific subject matter and/or professional assignment—special education, reading, gifted and talented education, and so forth.

5. Establish professional learning goals and continually assess progress and effectiveness of professional practice.

HOW TO USE THE PROFESSIONAL PERFORMANCE JOURNAL ■

Those who dare to teach must never cease to learn. (Socrates)

The professional performance journal in this instance is applied to PLC collaborations for professional development planning with a focus on an identified performance goal. The portfolio process is designed to provide a structure and process to identify the teacher's professional performance goal. To achieve their goal, they will determine gaps in their current repertoire to assist them in determining their focus for professional learning. If a beginning teacher or a teacher seeking a new credential has a coach/mentor, refer to the Learning Cycle of Teacher Development (see page 14).

To establish the conditions at the outset, it is helpful for participants to ask the following questions:

- Who will be facilitating the professional development portfolio process?
- How will they determine their professional development priority/focus?
- Who will be included in the decision process for designing and accessing the professional development requirements and opportunities?
- How will they collect artifacts and evidence of progress toward their goal?
- How will they communicate their outcomes and next steps?

Next, PLC members orient themselves as to how the professional performance journal process can serve as a guide for reflections and collaborations regarding their professional development and application of new instructional practices with students. The critical steps in beginning the process are

- establish a shared purpose;
- identify a banner question (the "big question" linking student needs with a targeted instructional priority);
- commit to several checkpoint meetings.

A checkpoint meeting is essential for monitoring progress and may include a roundtable discussion about member's work, observations, learnings, and questions that have emerged during the process.

Organization

Following is a model outline for the professional growth journal, reflecting the organizers of the process:

   I. Purpose

  II. Focus

     A. Banner question aimed at achieving professional goal and requirements

     B. Specific standards and requirement for achieving professional goal(s)

 III. Process

     A. Professional development plan—linked to professional goal and requirements

     B. Artifacts and evidence of professional learning progress

 IV. Outcome

     A. Reflection

     B. Exhibiting evidence of achieving professional goal(s)

Journal Design and Purpose

As detailed in the following, purpose, focus, process, and outcomes are the key components in the professional growth journal.

Why? (Purpose)

- To participate in a professional learning community
- To reflect on professional practices
- To share observations, learnings, and suggestions as part of the evaluation process

What If? (Focus)

- Generate a banner question (the "big question") for professional learning
- Identify specific area of professional performance goal(s)

How Will It Work? (Process)

- Make professional development plans
- Collect artifacts and evidence of professional learning and progress toward goal(s)
- Participate in professional development activities
- Implement new instructional practices
- Establish checkpoints to monitor progress toward goal(s)

So What? (Outcome)

- Demonstrate enhanced professional practices
- Report student achievement results
- Exhibit professional observations and learnings

As applied to professional development and the professional portfolio, the journaling process for educators consists of a series of actions that reflect purpose, focus, process, and outcome.

- Identify PLC members for collaboration.
- Participate in the introduction and initial purpose-setting session.
- Establish the banner question around an identified instructional priority.
- Build a professional development plan.
- Implement enhanced instructional practices.
- Determine a process to collect data (artifacts and evidence) to monitor progress.
- Report outcome results and evaluate the effectiveness of the process.
- Make adaptations in the process and practices, as indicated, for next steps.

CASE STUDY: PROFESSIONAL ■
PERFORMANCE JOURNAL

Following is an overview of the journaling process demonstrating the four phases outlined previously. This case study reflects the complete process and consists of journal pages and activities from actual professional development portfolio experiences. On the journal pages in this section, participants' responses are set in italics so that the various types of reflections prompted by the journaling process can be easily identified.

When you are ready to apply the journaling process for professional growth in your own PLC, note that the journal templates shown here are offered at the end of this chapter and on the accompanying CD. As you and your group start journaling to facilitate the professional portfolio process, you may refer to Professional Portfolios: Types and Purposes template in the Guides and Resources section at the back of the book and on the accompanying CD.

The first phase in the process is to define purpose and identify opportunities to explore in terms of the professional portfolio process (see Figure 5.1). This template serves as an organizer for reflections and discussions.

Figure 5.1   Why? (Purpose)

PURPOSE • PERFORMANCE • OUTCOMES

What is the purpose of the journal for professional performance portfolio?

The purpose is to participate in a professional learning community, reflect on professional practices, and share observations and learnings as part of the evaluation and credentialing process.

We will use the professional performance journal as a framework for initiating, planning, and facilitating our ongoing professional development, while connecting our purpose and focus for learning with the school community-at-large.

The professional performance portfolio will provide opportunities for us to

- identify credentialing requirements for a specific grade level and/or subject matter;

- focus professional development to expand your teachers repertoire;

- build and adapt a professional development plan;

- collect artifacts and evidence of required performance outcomes;

- collaborate with peers, as partners and in PLCs;

- sharpen professional management skills;

- apply leadership abilities;

- draw on past experiences and knowledge;

- observe and contribute to collegial development;

- assess the impact and influence of systemic change in our school;

- reflect on values, attitudes, and experiences.

As with the other structured journals for PLCs, the professional development journal is organized around four phases: purpose, focus, process, and outcome. At this time, the participants orient themselves to the entire process but concentrate on defining purpose—reflecting on why they are using the structured process. The group participants use the Learning Opportunities and Requirements template (Figure 5.2) to coach or prompt the reflective process, thereby determining the general theme for their portfolio work and building a sense of learning community.

Defining a professional credo is essential to this first purpose step in the professional growth journal process. The group participants in this study use the form in Figure 5.3 to facilitate reflection.

The next step in the professional performance journal process is to establish a focus for the professional development program and work

Figure 5.2   Learning Opportunities

Focus Development to Expand Your Teaching Repertoire

Identify an entry point for professional growth. Select an area of concern, interest, and/or expertise that is a priority for you and articulate it in the form of a banner question.

Build and Adapt a Professional Development Plan

Select learning activities that contribute to your learning (inquiry) process. Choose activities that can provide a variety of experiences and highlight interactions with individuals and ideas.

Collect Artifacts and Evidence of Required Performance Outcomes

Gather data and items for portfolios that represent development and reflect new understandings in terms of professional growth and achieving your performance goal(s).

Collaborate With Peers as Partners and in PLCs

Meet with a portfolio partner on an ongoing basis and in roundtable discussion groups with other participants in the learning community. Roundtable discussions may include colleagues who have similar learning priorities, consultants, and members of the school administration/school community who are involved in the process.

Sharpen Management Skills

Identify skills that may be involved with your banner question, choosing from the standard professional skills that help you get the job done.

Applying Leadership Abilities

Choosing from those features that are characteristic of effective leadership, identify abilities that are connected to professional growth and the portfolio process.

Draw on Past Experiences and Knowledge

Consider prior learnings and use them as a starting point for your inquiry as you form your banner question and build a professional development plan with your portfolio partner.

Observe and Contribute to Collegial Development

Create an environment in which every person is a teacher and every teacher a learner. (Throughout the journaling/portfolio process, you will have opportunities to collaborate and be both a learner and a teacher.)

Assess the Impact of Your Work on School Systems

Consider the systems within your school community that will support or interfere with the outcome of this professional performance portfolio process.

Reflect on Values, Attitudes, and Experiences

Meet with peers and, as a group, reflect in your journals on learning activities and classroom practices, selecting artifacts and evidence for inclusion in the process.

Figure 5.3   Defining Your Professional Credo

1.   **What are your beliefs about the purpose of your profession?**

I believe that it is my job to provide students with the skills necessary for both success in their chosen careers and lives in general. I feel it is my job to expose them to a wide variety of subjects and experiences in order to give them the opportunity to explore their interests and talents.

2.   **Describe the ideal curriculum.**

The ideal curriculum is a curriculum in which several disciplines are connected and address a variety of learning styles or intelligences, a curriculum that provides students with as many chances as possible to express themselves in a creative manner, and to experience success, a curriculum that offers students useful, relevant skills, and a standards-based curriculum that prepares students for on-going success as they progress through the grades

3.   **What are your beliefs about how students learn?**

I believe that students learn by using a combination of their intelligences. I especially feel that they learn best when they are allowed choices in how they express facts and concepts studied in the classroom. In addition, I believe the content presented must be meaningful and relevant to the students. Instructional practices should be differentiated to accommodate all learners.

toward their professional goal. Ultimately, a banner question will be generated as an essential question to focus their inquiry regarding their professional goal(s) and their plan for learning, collaboration, and reflection as the participants use journaling to facilitate this process.

As the participants in this case start the focus step, they reflect on their professional goal(s) and inquiry, connecting the general purpose of their work with the professional performance goals of their school system.

At this step of the process, the participants are mindful of the four organizers for the structured journal (purpose, focus, process, and outcome), as they concentrate on their focus for learning. Participants often use this as an opportunity to reflect with a portfolio partner, seeking to identify a focus for their particular professional goal(s) and plan. At this point, the group establishes a schedule for checkpoints (group meetings) for future conversations and collaborations that are integral to the journaling process. At their checkpoints, they will share new learnings and observations, pose clarifying questions, and make adjustment in their plan.

To facilitate the focus step, the group uses a graphic organizer such as a Venn diagram (see Figure 5.4) to organize reflections and coaching collaborations with portfolio partners. Each participant takes five to seven minutes to generate a list of actions that he or she *needs* to do and a list of those actions he or she *want* to do. The *need-to-dos* are actions aligned with the

Figure 5.4   Venn Diagram for Focus Step

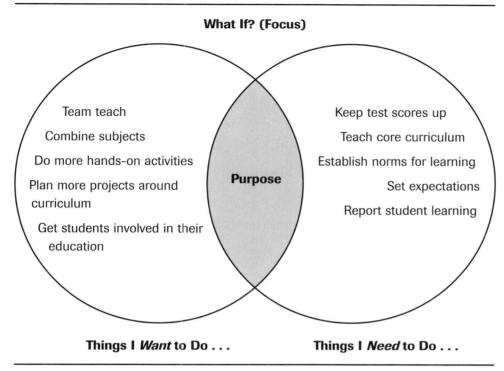

What If? (Focus)

Team teach

Combine subjects

Do more hands-on activities

Plan more projects around curriculum

Get students involved in their education

Purpose

Keep test scores up

Teach core curriculum

Establish norms for learning

Set expectations

Report student learning

Things I *Want* to Do . . .   **Things I *Need* to Do . . .**

state and/or local requirements for credentialing or evaluation. The *want-to-dos* are innovative or new actions individual members have an interest in doing—actions that, from their perspectives, would enhance their work.

After the lists have been generated, each participant takes five minutes to share his or her needs and wants with a partner, each taking a turn being a listener. The listener's role is to listen well enough to later pose thoughtful questions that will assist the partner in identifying emerging inquiries in regard to their goal(s). They are listening for clarity of ideas to be considered and possibly included in the plan for achieving their performance goal(s). Each participant endeavors to listen and ask questions of the partner, coaching that person in focusing on and clarifying their purpose and goal, *not* telling that person what he or she thinks.

The following templates can be found in the Guides and Resources section at the back of the book and on the accompanying CD; they will prove useful in this collaborative listening process so important to the focus step of the professional growth journaling process: A Guide for Listening and Directions for Coaching Triads.

After participants have identified their general goals in professional development, they use the banner question form (see Figure 5.5) to formulate the essential question that will guide their individual plans for professional development. The participants may refer to the Banner Questions Guide template to facilitate this process.

Figure 5.5   What? (Focus)

GOALS • REQUIREMENTS • INQUIRY

Banner Question

How do we create interdisciplinary instruction in our middle school?

Splinter Questions

What are the benefits of differentiated instruction?

How do we group students at present?

How can we pull in other disciplines (such as math with social studies)?

How can we facilitate student reflection?

How can we find a balance between process and content?

How should align instruction and materials with the content standards?

How can we address relevance of content to students?

How should we involve students in the assessment and learning process?

Establishing a banner question during the journaling process is not aneasy task, whether it is action research, the professional performance portfolio, PLC portfolio, the school portfolio, or the school reform portfolio. A New York City teacher-center facilitator once commented, "Banner questions are not written in stone—more like gelatin." Banner questions reform, change shape, and are flexible. Formulating *splinter questions,* which are smaller questions that constitute subsets of the proposed banner question, helps to guide and clarify the focusing process.

During this process, participants find it helpful to offer sample questions and share possible new questions. This strategy spurs thinking among members, encouraging each participant to formulate a banner question before proceeding to the process step of the professional performance journaling process.

When the group meets at this point, the individuals review their banner questions. Often these questions have changed from the last meeting—that is what continuous learning is all about. During a group meeting, they use the How Will It Work? (Process) form (Figure 5.6), as they begin to design a professional development plan.

At this time, the participants review the checkpoint dates (two or three meeting times scheduled in the future), which are important times for collaboration and sharing progress. To facilitate such meetings, the group uses the Professional Development Checklist template given in the Guides and Resources section at the back of the book and on the accompanying CD.

An important journaling activity for the professional performance portfolio process is the maintenance of a professional development log.

Figure 5.6   How Will It Work? (Process)

PLAN • DATA COLLECTION • COLLABORATION

- Make professional development plans.

- Collect artifacts and evidence of professional learning and student progress.

- Participate in professional development and credentialing activities.

- Implement new instructional practices.

- Establish checkpoints for monitoring student progress and teacher observations.

Professional Development Plan

Focusing on the development of a plan, establish collaborations to facilitate and support learning. Your professional development activities should be selected in terms of your specific performance goal(s) and individual classroom teaching situations.

The plan will contain your

- credo;

- banner question and professional performance goals;

- professional development and credentialing activities;

- outcome, as well as any refinements and applications to professional practices and achievement of professional performance goals.

The professional development plan will facilitate perusal and integrate learning from the inquiry. Begin with activities you are currently involved in and additional requirements for meeting your performance goals. Continue to add activities to your plan as you move through the portfolio process and collaborate with others. Some examples of professional development activities are

- visiting other schools;

- attending seminars;

- observing teaching and group facilitation activities in progress;

- meeting with other educators who share your interests;

- taking state exams to fulfill credentialing requirements;

- inviting a colleague to observe you at a meeting or professional workshop;

- reading articles from professional journals;

- joining a study group in the school community;

- researching a theme or concept related to your banner question.

Figure 5.7   Professional Development Log

MONTH	ACTIVITY	
August	*Professional Growth Journal/Portfolio Kick-Off.*	Purpose
September	*Banner question: Checkpoint all terms. Participate in orientation for credentialing program.*	
October	*Develop plan to work with portfolio partner and others who have similar performance goals.*	
November	*Meet with other teachers with similar performance goals. Look for common skills, concepts, and expertise to support each other in the learning process.*	
December	*First checkpoint meeting/process (round table) to share progress and learnings with PLCs.*	Focus
January	*Clarify opportunities to apply new learnings in day-to-day practices.*	
February	*Review time line regarding deadlines for meeting requirements to meet performance goals and submitting evidence of successful completion.*	Process (and Plan)
March	*Meet with portfolio partner to plan update progress.*	
April	*Review portfolio artifacts and evidence and share observations and feedback with portfolio partner.*	Outcome
May	*Review outcome at checkpoint meeting to conclude the professional performance/ portfolio process.*	

The group participants in this study use the Professional Development Log form (Figure 5.7) to facilitate this step, ultimately setting a schedule for professional growth and development—the portfolio process.

Next, the group moves to intensive collaboration with colleagues as part of the process step, using the Collaborations journal form (Figure 5.8) to reflect on the progress made.

Keeping track of the artifacts and evidence collected in the portfolio process is an important function. Group participants use the Artifacts and Evidence Registry (Figure 5.9) for this purpose.

The fourth step of the journaling process is articulating outcome. Participants in the group use the So What? (Outcome) journal form (Figure 5.10) to prompt thoughtful reflection.

Figure 5.8   Collaborations

When you meet with your colleagues during this stage of the professional performance portfolio process, reflect on your daily decisions and other experiences related to your inquiry. Discuss the integration and connections among the standards for your profession and if you have defined a common purpose for your work.

To facilitate collaboration

- discuss issues regarding performance outcomes for your credentialing;

- focus on banner question;

- consider professional development activities aligned with requirements;

- discuss recent experiences;

- share your professional development plan for evaluation and/or credentialing;

- plan to observe and/or meet with a partner;

- ask for feedback or input regarding a decision;

- make adaptations to your professional development plan;

- ask for suggestions regarding activities for your plan;

- research state requirements and assessments available to complete credentialing;

- exhibit artifacts and/or evidence of performance progress from your portfolio;

- share current findings or learnings;

- celebrate successful completion of requirements or evaluation outcomes.

Figure 5.9   Artifacts and Evidence Registry

Briefly list any artifacts and evidence, gathered for your professional portfolio, that prompt reflection or collaboration in relation to your banner question.

- *Notebook of research data about credentialing requirements*

- *Listing of state administered competency tests as part of fulfilling credentialing requirements*

- *Materials and resources for professional development activities*

- *Examples of student projects/student work*

- *Notes from principal, portfolio partner, and/or students*

- *Certificates of successful completion of state exams in your area of credentialing*

- *Record of activities and accomplishments by afterschool clubs such as the student council or homecoming celebration committee*

Figure 5.10. So What? (Outcome)

CONCLUSIONS • REFLECTIONS • REFINEMENTS • LEARNINGS

Reflecting back on the year, I have learned a great deal from working with my portfolio partner and teaching team. My banner question has given me focus and I have gained new understandings about my work, leading me to many conversations with colleagues. At times, I was unsure of the outcome and benefits—now I see so many possibilities.

The portfolio process helped to focus our collaborations. I got to know other staff members who participated in the portfolio process, and now better understand and appreciate their work.

I have come to realize the extreme effort it takes to build and sustain a PLC and the power of collaboration—coming to understand our many different needs, attitudes, performance goals, and teaching practices. That is, in fact, what makes the work of a PLC such a rich experience.

I have learned a lot from working with my banner question and professional performance goals this year. In many ways, I feel as if I have just begun, in terms of the collegial relationship I have solidified and the support I received from PLC members and my portfolio partner, I do not think I would have achieved my performance goals and fulfilled the necessary requirements with our their expertise and support. I plan to continue to support others in our PLC with this process.

What articulation, sharing, demonstrating, and exhibiting have you done in regard to your professional portfolio?

My team members and had a celebration and exhibited our evidence so successful completion of our performance goals. The best part of the celebration was reflecting on our learnings and our commitment to sustain or PLC in the future. We hope to gain more support and interest in expanding this idea with our fellow educators.

What new questions have emerged from your inquiry and development?

I would like take my current banner question to another level next year. A splinter question is how can we gain schoolwide support for using a portfolio process as part of our yearly evaluation? An additional question I have is why is there is such resistance to try new ways?

How have your beliefs or practices been challenged or changed?

I have been challenged by trying to find the time to meet and plan with team members. I know we are always pressed for time, but this kind of planning is very time-consuming. It will possibly take less time after we have become more experienced with the process.

What is a possible future banner question?

My portfolio partner and I are looking forward to going deeper with the implementation of new practices learned from our professional learning this year.

PROFESSIONAL PERFORMANCE WRAP-UP ■

Engaging in the professional performance portfolio process provides you with a framework for reflection on a scope of work and area of specialization for your teaching practices as you collaborate with colleagues. Isolation is a significant job hazard for the teaching profession, while sharing concerns, successes, and visiting other classes and schools opens new vistas for professional growth. Using journaling as a process in terms of your professional portfolio provides a way to focus on a particular interest or concern related to your work. Opportunities for reflection and collaboration with others in your professional community are the key benefits.

The professional performance journal process, based on the following four steps, serves as a guide to you and the learning community of which you are a part. Walking through the process once more, you

- start with a *purpose* (Why are you doing this portfolio?);
- identify a *focus* (What area of the teaching profession are you seeking to qualify?);
- design a plan or *process,* identify area of work and key requirements, and assess your current status to determine a work plan for achieving highly qualified teacher status in your area of professional work (How will you accomplish your professional development plan for highly qualified teaching?);
- reflect on an *outcome* (What have you learned and how will you attach your learnings to your work in the classroom?).

——HELPFUL HINTS——

Be patient with identifying your area of focus and your current status in regards to achieving highly qualified teacher status. Doing the research in regard to key requirements and identifying your current status to make a plan does take time. During the professional performance journal/portfolio process, it is not uncommon to discover you have uncovered a piece of work that is bigger than anticipated. Use your collaboration process with colleagues, a coach, or mentor to focus and modify your work along the way.

6

Professional Development Journal

Aligning With Instructional Priorities

I t is not enough to target staff development as a top priority for reform efforts. Leaders who are serious about educational reforms must take into account the nature of teachers as adult learners. (Moye, 1997, p. 7)

BACKGROUND OF PROFESSIONAL DEVELOPMENT ■

Traditionally, professional development within school districts has consisted of one-day inservice workshops on new educational theories and new methodologies or changes that have been mandated for the school community. Often those participating in and managing such workshops have expressed concern about the effectiveness of such staff development, questioning its worth and whether there is transfer of learning to actual classroom practices. In recent years, educators have questioned what effective staff development is and how they can determine its impact on student learning. It is important to note that over the years, the purpose, meaning, function, and design of professional development has changed. Viewing professional development, as it is today is aimed at accelerating student achievement—a framework for change—educators will find that the process addresses the needs of adult learners and supports the implementation and integration of new ideas into classroom practices.

Table 6.1   Student Performance Assessments

ASSESSMENT FORM	DESCRIPTION	PURPOSE
Observation	Teacher watches the students while they actively engage in the learning process and collects anecdotal information and evidence of their learning.	Provides an ongoing record of student approaches to learning tasks; may also give the teacher information needed to make appropriate interventions.
Peer Feedback	Students assess their classmate's work using journal responses, brief assessment sheets, and/or sharing specific examples from the work. Peer feedback requires structure and training for students. Scoring and comment sheets are forms of structure; teacher-provided focus questions are another form of structure.	Provides students with specific information that will help them improve their performance or product. Peer feedback also affords students the opportunity to perform for a larger audience and to broaden their understanding of how the particular task can be approached.
Rubric	A rubric is a scoring scale that shows specific areas of competency regarding a selected item of work. It defines differing levels of achievement regarding the particular task.	A rubric provides feedback to the student about a specific performance to further enhance learning. The most powerful rubrics are ones generated by the teacher and students as preparation and evaluation of a project or piece of work.
Exhibition	An exhibition may be reports, artifacts, or examples of work that demonstrate student progress and accomplishments with a particular area of learning. During an exhibition, the student shows their work in a formal presentation.	Like an art exhibition, this form of assessment is often the culmination of a large, complex study over time. High schools sometimes use exhibitions as one form of exit examination.
Demonstrations	Students may give a speech, presentation, or act in plays to demonstrate their understanding. Often students defend their work during a demonstration. A science experiment or demonstration also fits this category.	Demonstrations give students an opportunity to articulate what they have learned for a wider audience. Demonstrations also provide the teacher with insight into a student's learning and skills.
Illustrations	Illustrations may be charts, graphs, artwork, or photos that show a student's understanding and skill in graphic form.	Illustrations provide alternative ways for students to show evidence of their understanding of concepts and to demonstrate their skills.
Descriptions	Students describe their learning process and self-assess their progress toward a specific learning outcome. Descriptions may be in written form or in dialogue with the teacher. Some examples include problem solving in mathematics and science or analyzing a piece of literature.	Reflection provides a powerful learning tool. Descriptions allow the student to verbalize their own thinking process in relation to the task. Descriptions also provide the teacher with information regarding evidence of learning or specific areas of confusion.

As a professional learning community (PLC), you have an opportunity to optimize your professional collaboration ability to impact student learning by engaging in job-embedded professional learning, combined with opportunities to learn about new practices and emerging theories applied to today's educational system.

Some of these collaborative practices include

- classroom observations;
- looking at student work;
- paired teaching;
- book studies.

These professional practices inform our instructional decision-making process when applied in active teaching. Coupled with new information and program enhancements, PLCs can design a plan for new instructional practices that impact student learning.

Today's data analysis tools and standards with benchmarks support or establish a baseline of performance and identify an instructional need. This is then followed by monitoring progress and continually improving on the process to sustain student gains over time. This is the critical work of a PLC.

Analysis Tool—Connecting Evidence of Student Learning

We assess student learning using many different methods and we report multiple forms of student data for varying purposes. The most powerful forms of assessment enable the learner to have a clear understanding of what they are trying to do and to learn and permit the teacher to intervene appropriately in order to maximize the learning process. This, in turn, leads to success in performing on high-stakes testing. Table 6.1 provides descriptions of different forms of performance assessments that produce evidence of learning and might be included in the student's portfolio.

HOW TO USE THE PROFESSIONAL DEVELOPMENT JOURNAL ■

The traditional approach to helping educators learn has been to develop the skills of individuals to do their work. Staff development needs to enhance the collective capacity of people to create and pursue overall visions. (Senge, 1997, p. 9)

Using a structured journal to guide the professional development process can impact the long-range goal of professional development planning. Journaling is an effective tool for reflection, allowing teachers to use the professional development process effectively and to assess the impact of new teaching practices in the classroom.

Ideally, the decisions and designs in effective professional development plans are rooted in learner-centered theories and philosophical beliefs. The following principles, reflecting a teacher as learner approach, serve as guidelines to create effective professional development environments:

- Invite learners (professional educators) to use their creative abilities, talents, interests, and concerns as mediums to reach a deeper level of learning, involvement, and professional commitment.
- Use inquiry as a foundational tool to engage the learners, encouraging them to seek answers to their own questions as well as those posed by their colleagues.
- Facilitate the process by identifying the learners' current perceptions and levels of understanding in the context of a particular development plan, concept, theory, or concern. Use this data to make informed decisions about adapting and customizing the process.
- Allow opportunities for feedback, reflective writing, and collaborations in an effort to internalize conceptual understandings and build learning communities.
- Encourage learners to identify their entry points (strongest modes of learning) for planning and demonstrating the integration of new ideas into their classroom practices.

These principles for adult learning coupled with knowledge about the process of school improvement lead to staff development as a framework for change—one that provides opportunities for truly effective professional development.

In writing about professional development, Guskey (1994) offered the following attributes as considerations for results-oriented professional development:

- Recognize that change is both an individual and an organizational process.
- Think big but start small.
- Work in teams to maintain support.
- Include procedures for feedback on results.
- Provide continued follow-up support and pressure for continuous improvement.

In an article on professional development, Darling-Hammond (1996) addressed criticism of teachers today, pointing out that it is not a question of teachers not doing their jobs. The fact is that their jobs have changed. As in other professions, the new practices professional educators are being asked to employ require building capacity and working collaboratively for continuous improvement. It is important that teachers be supported in the learning process through effective professional development.

The process of journaling allows teachers to reflect on the learning process, assessing the impact of their professional development activities on classroom practices and student learning.

Organization

The structured journal process for professional development is built around the basic four phases: purpose, focus, process, and outcome. The PLC establishes roles and responsibilities around facilitating the work and archiving the stories, observations, and results of the process. Each learner (professional educator) keeps a journal of the process to sustain the focus of the PLC and support monitoring progress and reflections on learning and the impact on student achievement. The PLC begins their process by asking the following questions:

- **Purpose.** Why you are doing a professional development portfolio?
- **Focus.** What is the theme or focus for professional learning and how is it aligned with our instructional priorities?
- **Process.** How will we collaborate as a PLC to learn, practice, and reflect?
- **Outcome.** How will we know it is working and what we want to learn next?

Journal Design and Process

The purpose of the journal is to provide a framework for organizing, constructing, implementing, and reflecting on the PLC professional development plan. The following is a model for using the staff development journal, denoting the actions that characterize the four steps in the process.

Why? (Purpose)

- Establish the reason for the particular professional development plan and how it connects to the identified instructional priority.

What If? (Focus)

- Identify the instructional domain for professional learning.

How Will It Work? (Process)

Describe how you will

- analyze student data to determine instructional priority;
- determine the gap between current instructional practices and programs and identified student needs (instructional priority);
- construct a professional development plan;
- participate in professional developement, classroom observations, and PLC reflections and collaborations;
- implement new instructional practices;
- establish a process to monitor student progress;
- assess impact on student learning and make adaptations as indicated.

So What? (Outcome)

Conclude participation in the PLC professional development process with final reflections—report results and make recommendation for next steps.

- The primary purpose of staff development is to allow professionals working in learning communities to reflect on professional practices and connect new learnings to current practices. The professional development journal will focus and organize that process. The expectation is that participants will use the journal process, along with content knowledge, to work effectively toward change.

■ CASE STUDY: PROFESSIONAL DEVELOPMENT JOURNAL

This final reform—weaving continuous learning into the fabric of the teaching job—will be the one that makes the difference if we can act in a concerted fashion in every school and community to take the teaching job as it is now defined and confined and extend it into a true profession. (Renyi, 1996, p. 30)

Following is an overview of the journaling process, including samples of journals and activities from actual professional development experiences. On the journal pages in this section, participants' responses are set in italics so that the various types of reflections that are prompted by the journaling process can be easily identified.

When you as a facilitator or professional learning community member, are ready to apply the journaling process in your own professional development sessions, note that blanks of the professional development journal templates shown here are offered at the end of the book on page 92 and on the accompanying CD.

The journal pages can be presented and used in a variety of ways depending on the needs of the participants. All the journal pages may be introduced at the first session to orient the participants to the entire process, or the journal pages may be gradually introduced in a series of staff development sessions. If time allows, each development session may focus on one journal page at a time.

This case study represents a third-grade PLC. This PLC is comprised of all the third grade teachers and their support teachers, such as the reading specialist. They have made a commitment to use student data to determine the instructional priority, based on student needs for the term and to build their professional development plan around their identified instructional priority. In this case, it is reading comprehension.

The questions in the Why? (Purpose) form (Figure 6.1) regard the focus of PLC and professional development planning, prompting each PLC member to reflect on his or her role as a teacher, on their goals for the professional development in this particular case, and on his or her grade level instructional priorities.

The participants move on to the focus step with a review of the four parts of the journal (purpose, focus, process, and outcome). Using the

Figure 6.1   Why? (Purpose)

OBSERVATIONS • CONCERNS • QUESTIONS

1.   Describe the role of teacher as facilitator of student learning.

I think the teacher is a facilitator because he or she must listen to and observe the child. Therefore, the teacher is mediating or modifying curriculum to meet the needs of the child. This process is a two-way communication process. I consider that communication to be facilitation, rather than the perception some have about teaching as a one-way telling process.

2.   What do you see as the primary purpose of professional development?

We must begin with student's instructional needs. The first step is to analyze multiple sources of student data and determine what our instructional priority will be for the term. Based on the data analysis we will establish a grade level priority for professional development.

3.   What are your personal theories about how children learn?

I think children learn all the time. How they learn in school is another issue. They probably learn in school when they are interested and feel successful. This could require a variety of methods and modalities. The challenge is these methods should vary from child to child, which creates an even greater challenge when you have a large and diverse class.

4.   What are your instructional priorities?

Reading comprehension for expository text and vocabulary development are my top two instructional priorities.

After meeting with our grade level team and listening to faculty members from other grade levels, it appears that reading comprehension is a challenge for most of our students. For me it is a priority. My students would benefit from expository reading strategies to enhance their learning in all subject areas. They would also benefit from cognitive and structural analysis skills to expand vocabulary development.

What If? (Focus) form (Figure 6.2), the participants zero in on the application area for learnings from the staff development plan.

During this step of the process, the PLC members focus on and clarify the purpose of the professional development—in this case, a priority instructional area. At this point, site administrators and other staff members in the school community are invited to participate. They facilitate the sharing of information by responding to teachers' questions regarding the school community's long-term planning and desired outcomes or expectations. A staff developer (or sponsor for the development session) is present to support the learning/journaling process.

Moving to the third step of journaling, the participants use the How Will It Work? (Process) journal form (Figure 6.5). The participants decide to use this form at each staff development session to reflect and provide regular feedback to the facilitator. They also address the need to make

Figure 6.2   What If? (Focus)

DETERMINE INSTRUCTIONAL PRIORITIES

Step 1: As a grade level or subject matter team establish a process to analyze student data to determine priority area for instructional improvement.

Step 2: Organize multiple sources of student data in grade level and/or department teams

    a. Include standardized tests scores, program/publisher tests, classroom-generated tests, samples of student work and observations.

    b. See Table 6.1 for Student Performance Assessments

Step 3: Analyze student data and look for patterns, themes, and compelling "ah-ahs"

Step 4: As a staff or grade level/subject matter team, agree on 2–3 instructional priorities

Step 5: Use data to support recommendations for new instructional strategies

Step 6: Determine staff readiness to implement new practices and identify professional development needs.

    1. The instructional area I have chosen in which to apply learnings from this staff development is…

      It appears that our instructional priority will be literacy with a focus on structural analysis skills and reading comprehension.

    2. The professional development will alter my current practices, since…

      Currently, I have been concerned about my students' spelling, and I think the structural analysis will help both the reading fluency process and spelling. My students do not seem to be reading and comprehending independently. They seem to be dependent on visual cues and mediated conversations to be able to articulate their understanding of what they have read. I would like to participate in professional development activities that would give me new strategies to use with my students and formative assessments to monitor progress in spelling and reading comprehension.

adaptations with their instructional practices and to build an implementation plan. (See A List of Facilitation Strategies with the templates in the Guides and Resources section at the back of the book and on the accompanying CD.)

During the final step (outcome), the PLC members, in this case the site leadership team (SLT), meet with the entire staff to share the student results and professional learning reflections on the entire experience. This final session with the participants has been arranged ahead of time and,

Figure 6.4   How Will It Work? (Process)

PLAN • DATA COLLECTION • COLLABORATION

Complete records of learnings and impact from professional development activities.

Date: *April 9*

Session: *Reading Comprehension at Work*

I expected to learn…	I learned…
about how I might apply new comprehension strategies with my students.	*advanced organizers to assist students in establishing a frame of reference for understanding and retaining what they have read.*
I plan to…	Next time I…
begin to practice strategies with my students and see monitor their progress.	*would like to hear from others who have used the new strategies and their student progress.*

with the permission of all involved, copies of the completed So What? (Outcome) journal forms (Figure 6.4) are made available—this allows them to be reviewed by the learning community as a whole. The teachers, facilitators, and other participants look for patterns of learnings in the various responses while discussing the impact the sessions have had on classroom practices and implications for the school system's long-term planning. Checkpoint, Template 6.3, for monitoring progress is available on page 128.

Figure 6.5   So What? (Outcome)

CONCLUSIONS • REFLECTIONS • REFINEMENTS • LEARNINGS

What articulating, sharing, demonstrating, and exhibiting have you done with your peers in regard to your learnings?

Several colleagues have visited my class to observe my students in action with the new strategies I have learned in our professional development sessions.

What new questions about your study and strategies have emerged from participation in the staff development?

I now see a need for the cognitive frame setting prior to reading to support their reading comprehension.

How have your beliefs about student needs changed?

I am much more aware of individual needs and the importance of meeting those needs.

Future plans for using the new practices should include…

opportunities to observe and collaborate with fellow teachers.

■ PROFESSIONAL DEVELOPMENT WRAP-UP

There has been a growing interest in assessing the impact of professional development on student learning. Professional development has evolved from workshops that teach curriculum and programs, to learning communities that are committed to student learning outcomes. In light of this commitment, professional educators are now seen as teacher-learners.

The professional development journal provides a structure and process for reflecting on student achievement and professional practices—connecting learnings from professional development to your classroom. The learnings from the journal process can also serve as data or evidence of teacher development and student learning so the quality of the professional development and the connection to working with students may be assessed.

Using the structured journal as a guide, you

- identify a *purpose* for professional development;
- *focus* on a targeted instructional priority or standard;
- design a *plan* and *process* for implementing new practices in the classroom;
- consider the *outcome* of the professional development and collect evidence of the impact of your work on student learning.

——HELPFUL HINTS——

Use the PLC professional development journal to connect learnings to classroom practices and to give feedback to professional workshop instructors or sponsors. The journal can assist in making decisions regarding the design and ongoing support of future professional development activities.

Guides and Resources for Professional Learning Communities

PLC Resource Matrix

Resources	1 PLCs at Work	2 School Reform	3 Action Research	4 School Portfolio	5 Highly Qualified Teacher	6 Instructional Priorities
Systems Planning Model	√	√	√	√	√	√
Guide to Professional Collaboration	√	√		√	√	√
PLC Readiness Rubric	√	√	√	√	√	√
Banner Question Guide	√		√			
Strategy for Determining Priorities	√	√	√	√	√	√
Professional Development Checklist	√				√	√
Portfolios Types and Purposes	√	√	√	√	√	√
Student Performance Assessments	√	√	√	√	√	√
Student Profile Checklist	√					√
Directions for Coaching Triads	√				√	√
Facilitation Strategies	√	√		√		√
Guide to Listening	√	√	√	√	√	√
Thoughtful Questions for PLCs	√	√	√	√	√	√
Worksheet for Defining Purpose and Priorities	√	√	√	√		√
School Portfolio Survey	√			√		
Learning Cycle Text and Visuals	√		√		√	
Glossary	√	√	√	√	√	√
Journal Templates						
School Reform		√				
Action Research			√			
School Portfolio				√		
Highly Qualified Teacher					√	
Instructional Priorities						√

√ indicates alignment with chapter(s) as a valuable tool for them

Resource 1.1 Systems Planning Model

Systems Planning Model

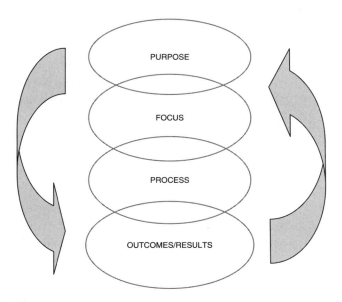

Resource 1.2 Organizers for the Systems Planning Model

PORTFOLIO JOURNAL PHASE	KEY ACTIVITIES	TOOLS AND STRUCTURES
Purpose for work	• Clarify purpose and how SLT will serve school reform purpose • Obtain leadership and Sponsorship for the work • Engage key stakeholders • Define roles and responsibilities	• Alignment on purpose • Establish Site Leadership Team (SLT) • Orient SLT to the Systems Planning Model and the Journal Process • Facilitation strategies
Focus for priorities	• Facilitate staff meetings to introduce process • Establish process for data analysis • Agree on instructional priorities in grade-level or subject-matter work teams	• Instructional priority setting process • Engage staff in data analysis and establishing an instructional priority • Engage faculty in identifying professional development needs to build capacity for instructional priority
Process for planning and monitoring progress	• Build action plan to implement new instructional practices • Establish professional development plan for implementing new instructional practices • Schedule check points to monitor progress	• Implement action plan and monitor progress • Implement professional development activities • Establish checkpoints with protocols • Collect learnings with artifacts and evidence of progress • Make adjustments in action plan according to check-point data
Outcomes for reporting results	• Assess and articulate results • Debrief lessons learned and impact of new practices • Report results to stakeholders • Decide next steps • Celebrate accomplishments	• Reflect on learnings from the process • Draw conclusions on results • Refine and archive collection of artifacts and evidence for reporting result

Note: These Key Activities are the most critical elements for establishing a sound foundation and organization to build the capacity and support the change process for school reform. These key activities contribute to building a professional learning community for change.

A Guide for Active Listening

GUIDE FOR PROFESSIONAL COLLABORATION ■

Constructivist collaboration is the action and interaction among willing participants that results in learning. It usually involves a combination of talking, listening, observing, doing, thinking, and reflecting. Collaboration can have a variety of purposes and is often initiated by a specific focus or need. The process of collaboration may lead to discovering new understandings, purposes, and needs.

Collaboration differs from simple discussion primarily in the purpose for the conversation. A collaboration would be a dialogue fueled by exploring an issue, in which questions such as *what if?*, *how about?*, and *why?* are posed—thus inviting new thinking and creativity. A discussion, on the other hand, would be a conversation that examines the pros and cons of a known quantity or fact.

Consider the purposes, processes, and outcomes of peer collaborations:

To discover

Listen in order to understand	Talk in order to listen
Listen in order to pose questions	Talk in order to explain or clarify

To invent

Listen in order to focus	Talk in order to interpret

To plan

Listen in order to empathize	Talk in order to invite reflection
Listen in order to rethink	Do in order to discover

Some examples of collaboration as a combination of interactions, actions, and purposes are the following:

Reflective Conversations

These conversations often include responses and interactions that help to clarify, summarize, focus, and hypothesize, as well as invite rethinking.

Critical Friend Conversations

These interactions are usually with colleagues or other individuals with whom you have a high level of trust, and with whom you can openly reflect, give and receive feedback, and restructure thinking.

Sharing and Supporting Conversations

These are opportunities to openly share emotions as well as receive acceptance and support. These conversations are usually initiated by sharing reactions and feelings related to a specific event or topic.

Roundtable or Debriefing

These conversations are aimed at communicating learning, rethinking, hypothesizing, and/or generating ideas directly related to an observed activity(ies).

THOUGHTFUL QUESTIONS FOR ■
LEARNING COMMUNITIES

The following are eight thoughtful questions that are useful when working with

- action research teams,
- professional portfolio "roundtables,"
- school/district leadership teams,
- school improvement committees,
- professional learning communities.

For each question, fill in the blank with the group's selected focus or priority.

- How does _____ impact student learning?

- How can _____ contribute to self-esteem?

- What evidence/experience do we have that _____ is important to the educational process?

- How might _____ change what you are doing?

- What are the implementation considerations for the proposed change?

- What capacities, understandings, and commitments are necessary to consider _____ ?

- What are the willingness and the readiness levels among staff members for considering _____ ?

- What are your suggestions regarding the proposal or issue?

■ WORKSHEET FOR DEFINING PURPOSE AND PRIORITIES

Agreement regarding the purpose, or alignment in terms of common purpose and desired outcome, is a critical starting point. It builds the foundation for effective design and implementation of school change efforts. Change efforts work best when shared purpose and priorities are clearly agreed upon from the beginning.

Such alignment provides

- the context for decision making,
- the yardstick for progress,
- the focus for collaboration and shared responsibility,
- the motivator for excellence and high performance.

Following are leading questions for defining shared purpose and establishing schoolwide priorities:

- From my perspective, the primary purpose for schooling...

- I see my major contributions to the school community as being...

- I will consider our change efforts worthwhile if the following things happen...

SCHOOL PORTFOLIO SURVEY ■

Reflect on and discuss the following statements, deciding whether you agree (A) or disagree (D) with them. The school portfolio group should work toward consensus as they take this survey.

1. School portfolios contain collections of artifacts and evidence representing growth and learning.

2. The portfolio process is so engaging that everyone catches on and is eager to participate from the start.

3. Checkpoints and feedback loops, designed to assess progress and refocus directions, are important to document in the school portfolio process.

4. Once there is agreement on the purpose and process for school change, the school portfolio framework should be easy to implement.

5. The school portfolio is essentially a scrapbook that tells a story.

6. School portfolios should come to a close at the end of each school term.

7. The school portfolio design, process, contents, and outcome will vary according to the purpose of the school portfolio.

8. The first step in designing a school portfolio is to collect data and then establish a purpose for the portfolio.

9. The portfolio process can enhance school and community involvement in the change process.

10. A rubric really drives the portfolio process.

Recommended answers: 1. A; 2. D; 3. A; 4. D; 5. A; 6. D; 7. A; 8. D; 9. A; 10. D

■ A STRATEGY FOR DETERMINING PRIORITIES FOR SCHOOL CHANGE

Purpose

To identify top priorities for improving student performance schoolwide and to determine priorities for goal setting for the school community.

Process

Step 1. Outline the purpose, process, and payoff (outcome) for the school portfolio process session by presenting an overview of a session. This is a prime opportunity to discuss the importance of community involvement. It is also a good time to establish a focus or entry point for school improvement. (Recommended time is five minutes.)

Step 2. Divide into smaller groups, five to eight persons in each. They may be formed according to interests or schools, or members may be randomly selected. Have the small groups address the following task:

Brainstorm what your top priorities are for school improvement/ change, such as literacy, technology, interpersonal skills, block scheduling, and so forth.

The groups should record their data on flip chart paper. (Recommended time is fifteen minutes.)

Step 3. The data are condensed into one specific list of priorities for all the groups. (This list may have ten to twenty items. Recommended time is five minutes.)

Step 4. With participants having compiled a condensed list of priorities for the entire school portfolio group, they now vote. Have participants prepare a numbered list on a master sheet of paper. Each number corresponds with one priority.

Each participant may vote three times for any three, any two, or just one of the items. Participants mark the list next to the selected item to indicate their votes. If one item in particular is a concern for them, they may choose to put three marks on one line, or two on one, and one on another, and so on. The greatest number of votes per item determines the top priorities for school change. (Recommended time is five minutes.)

Step 5. The results are immediate and provide the school community with a fair scan of the opinion on top priorities for school change efforts.

The group can now determine the readiness, structure, and entry point for designing an improvement (action) plan. It is important to keep in mind that not all items on the priority list will be addressed at the same time, and that the beginning point does not necessarily mean that other concerns will be neglected. (Recommended time is ten minutes.)

Payoff

Determining two or three priorities (areas) for goal setting for the school community.

STUDENT PROFILE CHECKLIST ■

Questions for Evaluators to Ask

1. What do we predict will be the skills, abilities, knowledge base, and attitudes that all students will need to be successful and fulfilled in the future?

2. What academic and behavioral outcomes should we be striving to instill in our students?

3. What should our priorities be in creating a learning environment to achieve these outcomes?

4. What specialized skills, attitudes, values, or abilities should our school programs include?

5. What do we view as the most important characteristics of a school that is devoted to both rigor and relevance?

■ PROFESSIONAL PORTFOLIOS: TYPES AND PURPOSES

Presentation Portfolio

A collection, resume, or album that represents an individual's accomplishments, learnings, strengths, and expertise. It can serve as an introduction for personal and professional opportunities highlighting the purpose and meaning of one's work.

Working Portfolio

A collection of assignments, artifacts, and evidence that fulfill prescribed competencies, standards, or outcomes. Outcomes for credentials, course participation, or other requirements established by mediators, teachers, or supervisors of one's work may be included.

Learner Portfolio

Provides a framework and process for *learner-centered decisions* and designs, connecting the learner's goals and purposes with those of his or her work.

A GUIDE FOR LISTENING ■

Levels of Listening

Level 1. Listen in order *to* sort information.
    Focused on understanding

Level 2. Listen *for* themes, categories, and clusters of ideas.
    Focused on identifying speaker's needs

Level 3. Listen *with* metaview (with the "big picture" in mind).
    Focused on needs, priorities, and commitment to action for the speaker

Conscious listening is being 100 percent present for the speaker.

■ DIRECTIONS FOR COACHING TRIADS

Form triads (groups of three) for purposes of collaborative listening and select roles for the first round. Complete three rounds during one session so each triad member will have an opportunity to experience all three roles listed in the following.

Role of Storyteller

Talks about the focus of learning for professional growth. Shares experiences and observations that prompted interest and/or questions.

Examples of activities that might have prompted learning include observations (an individual's class and/or other classes); seminars or workshops; videotapes; conversations with colleagues, parents, or students; readings; and samples of student work.

Role of Listener

Listens at three levels: to hear ideas and details, to hear in order to pose questions, and to hear in order to understand.

The listener is careful not to interrupt thinking on the part of the storyteller, asking questions only to clarify understanding. The listener's major function is to coach the storyteller and assist that person in clarifying the process in order to focus on a target area, to take action, or to resolve misunderstandings.

Role of Observer

Listens to the conversation and notes the process used by both the listener and the storyteller.

The observer takes notes regarding specific techniques he or she noticed. When the listening session for a round is complete, the observer offers feedback to the listener and to the storyteller.

BANNER QUESTIONS GUIDE ■

Sample Banner Questions

- Would student learning be enhanced if there were opportunities for creative exploration of individual interests/talents?
- How do I construct a thinking/meaning centered curriculum for all students that addresses the needs of all learners?
- How can I move away from letter grading/effort grading systems to one that communicates students' specific accomplishments?
- What causes children to be aggressive and strike out at other children?
- What are the various kinds of creative learning environments that provide less fragmentation and more integration between skill and content?
- How can I effectively integrate evaluation and assessment for successful and useful program evaluation?
- How can I meet the needs of academically challenged students and—at the same time—meet the needs of my more advanced students?
- Why do seventh-grade students get off track so easily when they move to a departmentalized, rotating schedule?
- What motivates eighth-grade students?
- Why is there such a difference between oral and written communication?
- How can I make learning relevant to high school students?
- How can we define or redefine academic rigor?

Your Banner Question

Splinter Questions

- How does your banner question relate to your work?
- What do you hope to learn?
- Who are your collaborator(s), partner(s), or study group teammate(s)?
- What resources and learning opportunities are you considering?

■ PROFESSIONAL DEVELOPMENT CHECKLIST

Portfolio Checkpoints for Building a Learning Community

Purpose

- Introduce portfolio purpose and process
- Formulate and share your professional credo
- Discuss issues, concerns, and interests

Focus

- Establish and share banner questions
- Ask structured interview questions
- Discuss splinter questions related to the priority

Process

- Identify entry points for learning using reflective collaboration
- Collect and reflect on learning activities
- Share artifacts and evidence

Outcome

- Share, reflect, and rethink
- Describe learnings
- Demonstrate and celebrate

A LIST OF FACILITATION STRATEGIES ■

Jigsaw. Process for reading, summarizing, and integrating text.

Each participant reads a portion of the text, shares information, and collects information from others as well.

Carousel. Design for collecting ideas, reactions, and suggestions surrounding a model, strategic plan, or event.

Post charts around the room; write responses, suggestions, observations, and ideas; then walk around to read, respond, and enhance comments.

Multimedia Metaphor. Catalyst for constructing, connecting, and comparing multiple frames of reference.

Show brief video clip or read literature selection to facilitate dialogue regarding the representational meaning in the metaphor.

Cut Story. Technique for reading aloud—as a team or with the entire group.

Paste text on index cards then hand out the cards and have the group assemble in the appropriate order. Read the message aloud to the rest of the group.

Consulting Line. Design for aligning and connecting expertise with problems in the room.

Have participants line up in two rows facing each other. Ask the persons on the left to share a concern or problem they are experiencing. Have the corresponding partners on the right act as consultants and offer suggestions, solutions, pose questions, and so forth. After about five minutes, have each consultant on the right move to the next person in line and interview that person. As the line moves, each person meets another consultant and gains additional suggestions and questions. After two or three rounds, have the persons on the left become the consultants. Repeat this cycle several times.

Walk the Talk. Pick a partner and take a walk.

Select a topic, problem, or essential question. Report back at a specified time to share conversations with the others. This activity provides an opportunity to take a break, move around, and collaborate.

Visual Dialogue. Tool for collecting and recording the learnings in the room.

This tool could be a graphic organizer such as a mind map, a web, a drawing, a list, a chart, and so forth. Have a recorder keep a log of the session for the group.

Fish Bowl. Group dynamics technique for listening to others.

While others look on to observe, summarize, and take notes, inner-circle members of a group respond to essential questions.

Think-Pair-Share. Process for reflecting, writing, and sharing.

People pair up and compare thoughts with others in the room.

Constructive Controversy. A process for engaging in conversation.

Selecting a controversial issue, group members express as well as listen to multiple points of view.

Journal Templates

Contents

The following templates are designed for reproduction for the reader's convenience.

Professional Performance Journal Templates   **116**

Professional Development Journal Templates   **126**

■ **SCHOOL REFORM JOURNAL TEMPLATES**

Template 2.2   Why? (Purpose)

PURPOSE • COMMITMENT • GOALS

1. From my point of view the primary purpose of our site leadership team is the following:

2. I bring the following expertise and commitment to our team efforts:

3. I will consider our site leadership team efforts a success if the following things happen this year:

Template 2.3 What? Instructional Priorities (Focus)

DATA • ANALYSIS • PRIORITIES

As an SLT, facilitate a staff meeting where each grade level or department shares its priority area for instructional improvement.

At a staff meeting, we introduced our four-phase process for determining instructional priority goals. We brought samples of student data to practice the data analysis process. We also set up a second session where we reported out, by grade level, areas we were considering for instructional improvement.

Four-phase data analysis process for determining instructional priority:

1. Organize multiple sources of student data in grade-level and/or department teams.

2. Include standardized tests scores, program/publisher tests, classroom-generated tests, samples of student work and observations.

3. Analyze data student data and look for patterns, themes, and compelling "Ahas."

As a staff, we determined that one area of instructional improvement all grade levels had in common was reading comprehension. For our first pass as working as a staff on instructional priorities, we decided to make reading comprehension a schoolwide priority.

4. The goal is to agree on two to three instructional priorities for the year.

Template 2.4 How? Action Planning (Process)

PLAN • LEARN • IMPLEMENT • MONITOR

Action Plan Table

The following table describes the planning model to assist with organizing the phases, activities, tools, and structures to design, facilitate, implement, and sustain school reform.

PHASE	PARTICIPANTS	KEY ACTIVITIES
PURPOSE PLC Serving as an SLT		
FOCUS Instructional Priority Goals		
PROCESS Action Planning Professional Development		
OUTCOMES Monitor Progress and Report Results		

Template 2.5 Checkpoint

1. Review your instructional priority goals.

2. Build action plan.

3. Clarify roles and responsibilities.

4. Establish professional development needs and plan.

5. Set expected outcomes for instructional priority goals.

Template 2.6   So What? (Outcome)

RESULTS • REPORTING • CELEBRATION • NEXT STEPS

Share a summary evaluation of progress with priority goals

Celebrate lessons learned and successes

Next steps

ACTION RESEARCH JOURNAL TEMPLATES   ■

Template 3.1   Why? (Purpose)

OBSERVATIONS • CONCERNS • QUESTIONS

- How will our action research community impact student achievement?

- When will we meet to do this work?

- How will we make decisions to take action on outcomes?

The action research journal provides a framework for identifying, planning, and facilitating research. It provides opportunities for

1. identifying a target area for research;

2. building a research plan;

3. collecting information;

4. collaborating with peers as research partners;

5. observing;

6. assessing impact of strategies used in target area;

7. refining practices;

8. reflecting on experiences.

Purpose Statement

Template 3.2 Observations

1. What are your observations regarding student learning?

2. Describe strategies and practices that have been effective and others that have not worked so well.

3. What are your interests and concerns about your work?

Template 3.3   What If? (Focus)

Banner Questions

- What do we know about student performance?

- What are we especially interested in improving?

- What innovations and interventions might we consider?

- What are some of our concerns in our school community?

Research Team Establishes a Research Target

Research Focus Discussion

Template 3.4 Research Target

What is the impact of class size reduction on student learning in the area of literacy development and reading in particular?

1. Action Questions

   What if…

   How about…

   How could I…

2. Collegial Connections

3. Strategies and Skills to Implement

   Our goal is…

   We need to address…

Template 3.5 How Will It Work? (Process)

PLAN • DATA COLLECTION • COLLABORATION

- When will we meet?

- How will we collect data?

- What process will we use for observations and information gathering?

- How will we share roles and responsibilities in the group?

Research Plan

- Strategies to be employed

- Implementation plan

- Data collection template

- Observations and reflective collaborations

- Refinements of the plan

Template 3.6 Research Plan Strategy Form

Preparation

Materials:

Methods:

Resources:

Implementation Schedule

August

September

October

November

December

January

February

March

May

June

Template 3.7   Data Collection Form

Collecting and Analyzing Multiple Sources of Data to Study the Impact of Action Plans

WHO (demographic data to be collected)

Number of Students:

Gender: M _____ F _____

Stable student population (over three years):

Attendance:

Other:

HOW (processing of data and strategies in research plan)

SO WHAT (outcomes—formal and informal data)

Other Outcomes

Surveys

Template 3.8 So What? (Outcome)

CONCLUSIONS • REFLECTIONS • REFINEMENTS • LEARNINGS

1. What hypotheses did you bring to your research target area?

2. How did the data collection support your learning?

3. What new questions have emerged from your research?

SCHOOL PORTFOLIO JOURNAL TEMPLATES ■

Template 4.1 Portfolio

School Name

School Portfolio Team Facilitator

Names of Team Members

_____

_____

_____

_____

_____

_____

Template 4.2 Guide for Defining Purpose

The school portfolio is an organizer for planning and reflecting on continuous school improvement. It is a framework for working together to identify school priorities and to exhibit student learning outcomes.

The school portfolio process provides a structure for

- facilitating change;

- working together as a staff and school community;

- organizing, planning, and assessing student outcomes;

- collecting artifacts and evidences;

- building community relationships;

- reflecting on values and attitudes;

- drawing on past experiences and knowledge;

- exploring possibilities;

- building new understandings about priorities.

To work toward defining a purpose, the school portfolio team members will

1. consider their definition of common purpose and formulate and share their philosophy, highlighting belief systems about the purpose and process of education;

2. learn about the portfolio process as a tool for organizing school planning;

3. build communication abilities and listening skills.

Template 4.3 Why? (Purpose)

OBSERVATIONS • CONCERNS • QUESTIONS

1. From my perspective, the primary indicators of student learning are…

2. My personal theory about how students learn is…

3. At our school, I am most proud of…

Template 4.4   What If? (Focus)

At the focus phase of the process, the school portfolio team will

1.   define the priorities for the school community;

2.   select the top six or eight priorities using the Action Priority Wheel (Figure 4.5);

3.   form priority work groups accordingly.

Ideally, each priority work group is a mixture of parents, teachers, and other school community members. The teachers can check in with colleagues regarding the collections of artifacts and program descriptions. The parents and other members can enhance the process with their various perspectives. The process of conversations and collaborations within these groups builds school community.

Template 4.5 Action Priority Wheel

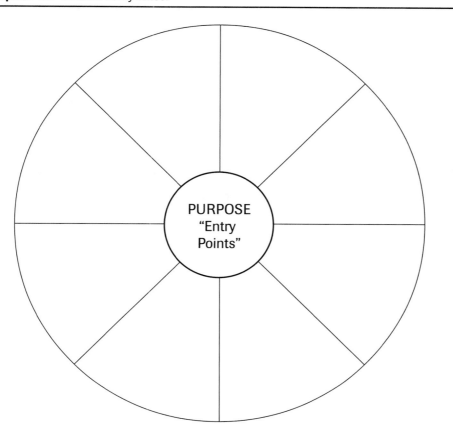

Template 4.6   How Will It Work? (Process)

PLAN • DATA COLLECTION • COLLABORATION

At the process phase, the team will

1. agree on a design and format for the school portfolio;

2. meet with community members in their individual priority action teams;

3. identify existing and future programs and practices that contribute to the various priorities;

4. consider future programs and practices to support priorities for change;

5. describe impact of existing programs;

6. collect artifacts and evidences of accomplishments;

7. agree on a plan for checkpoints (meetings to ascertain progress), as well as a time line for completion of the school portfolio.

Template 4.7   Priority Action Team Worksheet

Priority Description

Current Accomplishments

Future Plans and Suggestions

Template 4.8 Artifacts and Evidence Registry

Briefly list here any artifacts and evidence that represent actions for the selected priority.

Priority:

Template 4.9 So What? (Outcome)

CONCLUSIONS • REFLECTIONS • REFINEMENTS • LEARNINGS

1. Prepare the final product (the school portfolio) to be displayed at the school site.

2. Each priority team will contribute descriptions of programs and practices as well as the purpose for each priority section in the school portfolio binder. Members will also include artifacts and evidence of priorities and future plans.

3. The portfolio will be exhibited to the entire school community and will continue to serve as a presentation or album portfolio for orienting new families to the school.

4. Each year the portfolio can be revisited and updates can be added to reflect the process of continual school improvement.

■ PROFESSIONAL PERFORMANCE JOURNAL TEMPLATES

Template 5.1 Why? (Purpose)

PURPOSE • PERFORMANCE • OUTCOMES

What is the purpose of the journal for professional performance portfolio?

The professional performance portfolio will provide opportunities for us to

- identify credentialing requirements for a specific grade level and/or subject matter;

- focus professional development to expand your teachers repertoire;

- build and adapt a professional development plan;

- collect artifacts and evidence of required performance outcomes;

- collaborate with peers, as partners and in PLCs;

- sharpen professional management skills;

- apply leadership abilities;

- draw on past experiences and knowledge;

- observe and contribute to collegial development;

- assess the impact and influence of systemic change in our school;

- reflect on values, attitudes, and experiences.

Template 5.2 Learning Opportunities

Focus Development to Expand Your Teaching Repertoire

Identify an entry point for professional growth. Select an area of concern, interest, and/or expertise that is a priority for you and articulate it in the form of a banner question.

Build and Adapt a Professional Development Plan

Select learning activities that contribute to your learning (inquiry) process. Choose activities that can provide a variety of experiences and highlight interactions with individuals and ideas.

Collect Artifacts and Evidence of Required Performance Outcomes

Gather data and items for portfolios that represent development and reflect new understandings in terms of professional growth and achieving your performance goal(s).

Collaborate With Peers as Partners and in PLCs

Meet with a portfolio partner on an ongoing basis and in roundtable discussion groups with other participants in the learning community. Roundtable discussions may include colleagues who have similar learning priorities, consultants, and members of the school administration/school community who are involved in the process.

Sharpen Management Skills

Identify skills that may be involved with your banner question, choosing from the standard professional skills that help you get the job done.

Applying Leadership Abilities

Choosing from those features that are characteristic of effective leadership, identify abilities that are connected to professional growth and the portfolio process.

Draw on Past Experiences and Knowledge

Consider prior learnings and use them as a starting point for your inquiry as you form your banner question and build a professional development plan with your portfolio partner.

Observe and Contribute to Collegial Development

Create an environment in which every person is a teacher and every teacher a learner. (Throughout the journaling/portfolio process, you will have opportunities to collaborate and be both a learner and a teacher.)

Assess the Impact of Your Work on School Systems

Consider the systems within your school community that will support or interfere with the outcome of this professional performance portfolio process.

Reflect on Values, Attitudes, and Experiences

Meet with peers and, as a group, reflect in your journals on learning activities and classroom practices, selecting artifacts and evidence for inclusion in the process.

Template 5.3 Defining Your Professional Credo

1. What are your beliefs about the purpose of your profession?

2. Describe the ideal curriculum.

3. What are your beliefs about how students learn?

Template 5.4   Venn Diagram for Focus Step

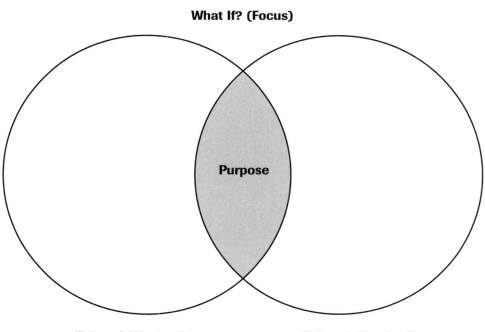

What If? (Focus)

Purpose

Things I *Want* to Do . . .   **Things I *Need* to Do . . .**

Template 5.5 What? (Focus)

GOALS • REQUIREMENTS • INQUIRY

Banner Question

Splinter Questions

Template 5.6   How Will It Work? (Process)

PLAN • DATA COLLECTION • COLLABORATION

- Make professional development plans.

- Collect artifacts and evidence of professional learning and student progress.

- Participate in professional development and credentialing activities.

- Implement new instructional practices.

- Establish checkpoints for monitoring student progress and teacher observations.

Professional Development Plan

Focusing on the development of a plan, establish collaborations to facilitate and support learning. Your professional development activities should be selected in terms of your specific performance goal(s) and individual classroom teaching situations.

The plan will contain your

- credo;

- banner question and professional performance goals;

- professional development and credentialing activities;

- outcome, as well as any refinements and applications to professional practices and achievement of professional performance goals.

The professional development plan will facilitate perusal and integrate learning from the inquiry. Begin with activities you are currently involved in and additional requirements for meeting your performance goals. Continue to add activities to your plan as you move through the portfolio process and collaborate with others. Some examples of professional development activities are

- visiting other schools;

- attending seminars;

- observing teaching and group facilitation activities in progress;

- meeting with other educators who share your interests;

- taking state exams to fulfill credentialing requirements;

- inviting a colleague to observe you at a meeting or professional workshop;

- reading articles from professional journals;

- joining a study group in the school community;

- researching a theme or concept related to your banner question.

Template 5.7   Professional Development Log

MONTH	ACTIVITY	
August		
September		Purpose
October		
November		
December		Focus
January		
February		Process (and Plan)
March		
April		Outcome
May		

Template 5.8 Collaborations

When you meet with your colleagues during this stage of the professional performance portfolio process, reflect on your daily decisions and other experiences related to your inquiry. Discuss the integration and connections among the standards for your profession and if you have defined a common purpose for your work.

To facilitate collaboration

- discuss issues regarding performance outcomes for your credentialing;
- focus on banner question;
- consider professional development activities aligned with requirements;
- discuss recent experiences;
- share your professional development plan for evaluation and/or credentialing;
- plan to observe and/or meet with a partner;
- ask for feedback or input regarding a decision;
- make adaptations to your professional development plan;
- ask for suggestions regarding activities for your plan;
- research state requirements and assessments available to complete credentialing;
- exhibit artifacts and/or evidence of performance progress from your portfolio;
- share current findings or learnings;
- celebrate successful completion of requirements or evaluation outcomes.

Template 5.9 Artifacts and Evidence Registry

Briefly list any artifacts and evidence, gathered for your professional portfolio, that prompt reflection or collaboration in relation to your banner question.

Template 5.10   So What? (Outcome)

CONCLUSIONS • REFLECTIONS • REFINEMENTS • LEARNINGS

What articulation, sharing, demonstrating, and exhibiting have you done in regard to your professional portfolio?

What new questions have emerged from your inquiry and development?

How have your beliefs or practices been challenged or changed?

What is a possible future banner question?

■ PROFESSIONAL DEVELOPMENT JOURNAL TEMPLATES

Template 6.1   Why? (Purpose)

OBSERVATIONS • CONCERNS • QUESTIONS

1. Describe the role of teacher as facilitator of student learning.

2. What do you see as the primary purpose of professional development?

3. What are your personal theories about how children learn?

4. What are your instructional priorities?

Template 6.2 What If? (Focus)

DETERMINE INSTRUCTIONAL PRIORITIES

Step 1: As a grade level or subject matter team establish a process to analyze student data to determine priority area for instructional improvement.

Step 2: Organize multiple sources of student data in grade level and/or department teams

    a. Include standardized tests scores, program/publisher tests, classroom-generated tests, samples of student work and observations.

    b. See Table 6.1 for Student Performance Assessments

Step 3: Analyze student data and look for patterns, themes, and compelling "ahas"

Step 4: As a staff or grade level/subject matter team, agree on 2–3 instructional priorities

Step 5: Use data to support recommendations for new instructional strategies

Step 6: Determine staff readiness to implement new practices and identify professional development needs.

    1. The instructional area I have chosen in which to apply learnings from this staff development is…

    2. The professional development will alter my current practices, since…

Template 6.3 Checkpoint

1. Review your instructional priority goals.

2. Build action plan.

3. Clarify roles and responsibilities.

4. Establish professional development needs and plan.

5. Set expected outcomes for instructional priority goals.

Template 6.4   How Will It Work? (Process)

PLAN • DATA COLLECTION • COLLABORATION

Complete records of learnings and impact from professional development activities.

Date:

Session:

I expected to learn…	I learned…

I plan to…	Next time I…

Template 6.5 So What? (Outcome)

CONCLUSIONS • REFLECTIONS • REFINEMENTS • LEARNINGS

What articulating, sharing, demonstrating, and exhibiting have you done with your peers in regard to your learnings?

What new questions about your study and strategies have emerged from participation in the staff development?

How have your beliefs about student needs changed?

Future plans for using the new practices should include...

Glossary

Action research. Educators researching in schools settings. Learning community members pose questions regarding their practice, focusing their inquiry through their daily practices. In action research, teachers draw questions from the classroom or from dilemmas that exist beyond the classroom door. The power of collaboration and reflection enhances the connections between classroom practices and research.

Artifact registry. Part of the structured journal where the teacher records the artifacts and evidence compiled in the portfolio, keeping track if, when, and why they are removed.

Artifacts. In terms of the portfolio and the journaling process, items that reflect who you are, what you do, what is important to you, and what your major interests are.

Change facilitation. The process of building capacity for having conversations that assist in forming attitudes and establishing norms which support members of a learning community through the transitions of change.

Checkpoints. Features of the portfolio process such as artifacts and evidences, partner meetings, individual induction plans, activities, and professional credo. These points serve as catalysts for discussion (and journaling) about the progress and success of the portfolio process.

Coevolving systems. Recognition of the interdependence of actions, attitudes, and the establishment of structures in a system. There are long-term and short-term influences as well as effects of actions on the system. The system is always in the process of evolving (changing/becoming) as are the participants in the system.

Collaborations. The group processes in which school community members participate during the school term; for example, study groups, seminars, peer coaching groups, and the sharing of experiences and learnings by professional portfolio users.

Collegial collaborations. Conversations, reflections, dialogues, and decision making that involve deep levels of understanding, commitment, reflection, and honesty—collaborations where assumptions are suspended and intentions articulated. The purpose for the collaboration invites questioning practices and construction of new understandings.

Community. A collection of individuals with a shared purpose in a climate of caring; an environment in which open communication, interdependence, and reciprocal processes are accepted as the norm.

Constructivism. The theory that knowledge should be *constructed* by the learner rather than being transferred from the teacher to the learner; a way to make meaning by interfacing with people, objects, and ideas.

Constructivist leadership. The reciprocal process that enables participants in an educational community to construct meanings that lead toward a common purpose about schooling (Lambert, 1995, p. 29).

Constructivist teaching. A teaching methodology that focuses on creating environments where learners can discover, construct, invent, and restructure knowledge. Simply put, if learning is knowledge constructed through experiences, and then constructivist teaching facilitates the learning process through experiences.

Contributors. In the context of frameworks for change, smaller ideas that require more detailed consideration, and emerge through the inquiry process of perusing a priority for learning.

Credo. A statement that reflects a current belief system.

Disequilibrium. In a learning community, an instance when the learner begins to sense contradictions in community members' reasoning or in existing structures—when ideas break down and then, ideally, are eventually reorganized into new thought patterns and structures.

Evaluation. An assessment of a process to find out if that process is serving its identified purpose. Ideally, measurements that determine success can be agreed upon—from the beginning—by all of those involved in the process.

Evidence. A document or documents that represent the educator's current level of expertise and professional engagement. Evidence may include credentials, letters of recommendation, students' work, and so forth.

Feedback. Information provided to another about what he or she has said or done. This information helps to clarify and respond to what has been observed or heard.

Frame of reference. The multiple perspectives that contribute to one's perception of what is, and the understanding of people, events, ideas, and actions. The frame of reference is based on the individual's experiences, histories, knowledge base, and capacity to listen and learn.

Individual learning plan. A design that contains activities, goals, and development suggestions to support and assist the teacher.

Instructional practices. The strategies, techniques, and processes teachers employ in facilitating learning with their students.

Journal. In the context of frameworks for change, a process designed to guide teachers as they participate in learning communities, as well as build and implement their professional development plans (portfolios). The process features opportunities for structured journal entries and recording of reflections, observations, and learnings—designed to share with peers, supervisors, and other community members.

Learner portfolio. A collection of artifacts and evidence that represent the current level of performance of the learner. The purpose is identified by the teacher-learner and influences the structure and process for the portfolio.

Learning community. A reference to the processes and relationships among group members that enable the entire community to learn and change. These processes and relationships include inquiry, dialogue, reflection, and action.

Learning cycle model. Designed for professional learning, a process for determining appropriate learning activities in order to construct new and deeper understandings (see Introduction).

Learning organization. An organization comprised of learning communities—communities where members are adaptive, generative, and creative learners. Groups of individuals that have come together with a shared purpose and agree to construct new understandings. "[A] place where people continually expand their capacity to create the results they truly desire, where new and expansive patterns of thinking are nurtured, where collective aspiration is set free, and where people are continually learning how to learn together" (Senge, 1990, p. 24).

Living systems. Systems that include living organisms, contributors to the function, maintenance, and evolution of the system and its members. A living system has the ability to adapt, restructure, evolve, reform, and regenerate contributors and members of the system.

Mechanistic system. A system that is machine-like, hierarchical, and designed to preserve the status quo.

Mental maps. The collection of ideas, experiences, and emotional development of an individual, which all contribute to the structures called upon to interpret and perceive events, information, and new ideas. Sometimes referred to as *frame of reference* or *point of view.*

Modify. To alter, adapt, or change a process or design in order to better serve the agreed upon purpose.

Partner meeting. In the professional growth framework, an opportunity for the teacher to meet with his or her partner and (1) share entries and deletions in the artifact registry; (2) discuss current professional development activities; (3) update the professional portfolio priority/focus; and (4) collaborate regarding progress and possible modifications in the individual learning plan.

Peer coaching. Pairs of teachers taking turns observing each other for the purpose of planning, designing, and refining their curriculum and instructional practices; also, a confidential process through which teachers share their expertise and provide one another with feedback, support, and assistance for the purpose of refining present skills, learning new skills, and/or solving classroom-related issues.

Point of view. The perception in one's frame of reference or mental model for perceiving and interacting. It influences the assumptions individuals make about their own intentions and actions as well as those of others.

Portfolio partner. In the professional growth framework, a colleague with whom the portfolio user meets on a regular basis in order to share and reflect on items in the portfolio as well as activities in the professional development plan.

Portfolio priority. An essential theme or focus in the professional portfolio process; a special interest or concern that the portfolio user has in terms of instructional practices and student outcomes; for example, class structure, grouping students effectively, variations for lesson designs, or block scheduling.

Professional communities. In the larger school community, those groups that primarily concern educators in their shared work of professional development.

Professional development activities. Learning opportunities that are included in the teacher's individual learning plan; for example, a course at a local university, staff development sessions at school, seminars that fit into the plan, observations of others' teaching, peer coaching participation, or selected professional readings (books/articles).

Professional development cycle. A model for identifying patterns of teacher development; a guide to identify where a teacher might be in the career cycle and what he or she needs to do to keep on growing as a professional (see Introduction).

Professional development plan. A collection of activities that relate to the teacher's focus for learning and to the general (schoolwide) goals for the school.

Professional growth portfolio. A process (framework for change) that provides educators with a structure or cognitive tool for initiating, planning, and facilitating personal/professional growth, while building connections between their personal interests and goals and those of the school.

Professional teachers. Those committed to first doing no harm; educators who continually seek more effective practices and revisit their purposes for schooling. Professional teachers facilitate learning for their students, honoring the individual's point of view and posing questions to help students find relevance to their learning. Professional teachers engage in leadership at many levels in the school system and are committed to building community.

Relationships. The interactions that inform individuals as to who they are and contribute to forming purpose and meaning in life. Relationships can provide support and caring in a community or they can be destructive and painful, depending on the varying contexts (home, school, etc.) and individual needs, capacities, and fears.

School communities. Those institutions or organizations with open boundaries of membership; including educators, children and their families, school board members, community leaders, local businesspeople, and other members of the larger community.

School portfolio. A process (framework for change) used as a communication method to report on the status of school programs and student progress to the community at large; also used as a way to celebrate accomplishments and plan for the future. A flexible tool, the portfolio can be used as part of the process schools go through as they apply for educational grants.

Study group. A framework for change; a collection of individuals who share a common interest or need for inquiry. The study group participants make a commitment to work together to support their colleagues' learning, forming effective collaborations along the inquiry path. Often a study group in a school community forms to read and reflect on a professional/educational book that includes information pertinent to the group members, or one that reflects a shared interest.

Zone of proximal development. The area in which one can learn with the support and/or mediation of a mediator or fellow learner; often referred to as one's instructional level, entry point, or zone for learning (Vygotsky, 1962).

References

Armstrong, T. (1994). *Multiple intelligences in the classroom.* Alexandria, VA: Association for Supervision and Curriculum Development.

Bailey, S. (Writer). (1995). *Structured dialogue: Inserting new cultural norms one conversation at a time. Association for Supervision and Curriculum Development presents: Satellite broadcast with Suzanne Bailey—Part II* [Motion picture]. Available from the Association for Supervision and Curriculum Development, Alexandria, VA.

Bailey, S. (1996). *Facilitation in the 21st century?* Danville, CA: Systems Guides Development Session.

Bernhardt, V. L. (1994). *The school portfolio: A comprehensive framework for school improvement.* Princeton, NJ: Eye on Education.

Block, P. (1993). *Stewardship: Choosing service over self-interest.* San Francisco: Berrett-Koehler.

Bridges, W. (1991). *Managing transitions: Making the most of change.* Menlo Park, CA: Addison-Wesley.

Brooks, M. G., and Grennon-Brooks, J. (1987, Fall). Becoming a teacher for thinking: Constructivism, change, and consequence. *Journal of Staff Development, 8*(3).

Brooks, M. G., and Grennon-Brooks, J. (1999). *In search of understanding: The case for constructivist classrooms.* Alexandria, VA: Association for Supervision and Curriculum Development.

Brooks, M. G., and Grennon-Brooks, J. (2000). *In search of understanding: The case for constructivist classrooms* (2nd ed.) Alexandria, VA: Association for Supervision and Curriculum Development.

Canning, C. (1991, March). What teachers say about reflection. *Educational Leadership,* 18–21.

Capra, F. (1982). *The turning point.* New York: Simon & Schuster.

Churchland, P. (1995). *The engine of reason, the seat of the soul.* Cambridge, MA: MIT Press.

Costa, A. L., & Kallick, B. (Eds.). (1995). *Assessment in the learning organization: Shifting the paradigm.* Alexandria, VA: Association for Supervision and Curriculum Development.

Covey, S. (1990). *Principle-centered leadership.* Hamden, CT: Fireside Press.

Darling-Hammond, L. (1996). What matters most: A competent teacher for every child. *Phi Delta Kappan, 78*(3), 198–200.

Dietz, M. E. (1991). *Professional development portfolio: A site-based professional development program.* San Ramon, CA: Frameworks.

Dietz, M. E. (1993). *Professional development portfolio: A constructivist approach to teacher development.* Paper presented at the Annual Conference of Critical Thinking, Massachusetts Institute of Technology, Boston.

Dietz, M. E. (1994, Spring/Summer). Facilitating for systemic change. *The Networker California Staff Development Council, 5*(4), 2–5.

Dietz, M. E., Green, N., & Piper, J. (1998). *Facilitating learning communities: Facilitator's manual.* Oxford, OH: National Staff Development Council.

Dolan, P. (1994). *Restructuring our schools: A primer on systemic change.* Kansas City, MO: Within Systems and Organization.

Edgerton, R., Hutchings, P., & Quinlan, K. (1991). *The teaching portfolio: Capturing the scholarship in teaching.* Washington, DC: American Association for Higher Education.

Fosnot, C. T. (1992). *Learning to teach, teaching to learn: Center for constructivist teaching/teacher preparation project.* Paper presented at the Annual Conference of the American Educational Research Association, San Francisco.

Fullan, M. (1991). *The new meaning of educational change.* New York: Teachers College Press.

Gardner, H. (1991). *The unschooled mind.* New York: Basic Books.

Glasser, W. (1993). *The quality school teacher: A companion volume to quality schools.* New York: HarperCollins.

Glickman, C. (1993). *Renewing America's schools: A guide for school based action.* San Francisco: Jossey-Bass.

Graves, S. S. (1996). *An examination of the value of the professional development portfolio: A conceptual framework for professional growth.* Unpublished doctoral dissertation, University of Ohio, Athens.

Guskey, T. R., & Sparks, D. (1996, Fall). Exploring the relationship between staff development and improvements in student learning. *Journal of Staff Development, 17*(4), 34–37.

Hord, S. M. (1997). *Professional learning communities: Communities of continuous inquiry and improvement.* Austin, TX: South West Educational Lab.

Hyerle, D. (1996). *Visual tools for constructing knowledge.* Alexandria, VA: Association for Supervision and Curriculum Development.

Johnson, M. J., & Bulton, K. (1998, November). Action research paves the way for continuing improvement. *Journal of Staff Development, 19*(1), 48–51.

Joyce, B., & Showers, B. (2002). *Student achievement through staff development.* Alexandria, VA: Association for Supervision and Curriculum Development.

Joyce, B., Wolf, J., & Calhoun, E. (1993). *The self-renewing school.* Alexandria, VA: Association for Supervision and Curriculum Development.

Katzenmeyer, M., & Moller, G. (1996). *Awakening the sleepy giant, leadership development for teachers.* Thousand Oaks, CA: Corwin Press.

Killion, J. P., & Todnem, G. R. (1991, March). A process for personal theory building. *Educational Leadership, 48,* 14–16.

Krupp, J. (1991, Fall). Beyond the 3 Rs: Focusing on quality of life. *Journal of Staff Development, 12*(4), 20–23.

Lambert, L., Collay, M., Kent, K., & Richert, A. E. (1996). *Who will save our schools: Teachers as constructivist leaders.* Thousand Oaks, CA: Corwin Press.

Lambert, L., Walker, D., Zimmerman, D. P., Cooper, J. E., Lambert, M. D., Gardner, M. E., et al. (1995). *The constructivist leader.* New York: Teachers College Press.

Mamchur, C. (1996). *Cognitive type theory and learning style.* Alexandria, VA: Association for Supervision and Curriculum Development.

McCarthy, K. W. (1992). *The on-purpose person.* Colorado Springs, CO: Pinon Press.

McLaughlin, M., & Vogt, M. E. (1996). *Portfolios in teacher education.* Newark, DE: International Reading Association.

Millman, J., & Darling-Hammond, L. (Eds.). (1996). *The new handbook of teacher evaluation: Assessing elementary and secondary school teachers.* Newbury Park, CA: Corwin Press.

Moye, V. H. (1997). *Conditions That Support Transfer For Change.* Thousand Oaks, CA: Corwin Press.

Owen, J., Cox, P., & Watkins, J. (1994). *Genuine reward: Community inquiry into connecting learning, teaching, and assessing.* Andover, MA: The Regional Laboratory.

Poplin, M. (1994). *Voices from the inside: A report on schooling from inside the classroom.* Claremont, CA: The Institute for School. Regional Laboratory for Educational Improvement for the North East and Islands.

Regional Laboratory for Educational Improvement for the North East and Islands. (1994). *Creating new visions for schools: Activities for educators, parents, and community members.* Andover, MA: Author.

Reiman, A. J., & Thies-Sprinthall, L. (1993). Promoting the development of mentor teachers: Theory and research programs using guided reflection. *Journal of Research and Development in Education, 26*(3), 179–185.

Renyi, J. (1996). *Teachers take charge of their learning: Transforming professional development for student success.* Washington, DC: National Foundation for the Improvement of Education.

Richert, A. E. (1994, April). *The culture of inquiry and the challenge of change: Teacher learning and the school change context.* Paper presented at the Spencer Foundation Fellows Forum, New Orleans, LA.

Rosenholtz, S. J. (1991). *Teachers' workplace: The social organization of schools.* New York: Teachers College Press.

Sagor, R. (1990). *Collaborative action research.* Washington, DC: Association for Supervision and Curriculum Development.

Schmoker, M. (1996). *Results: The key to continuous school improvement.* Alexandria, VA: Association for Supervision and Curriculum Development.

Schmuck, R. A. (1997). *Practical Action Research for Change.* Thousand Oaks, CA: Corwin Press.

Senge, P. M. (1990). *The fifth discipline: The art and practice of the learning organization.* New York: Doubleday.

Senge, P. M. (1997). The tragedy of our times. In V. Anderson & L. Johnson (Eds.), *Systems thinking basics: From concepts to causal loops*, 9. Waltham, MA: Pegasus Communications.

Senge, P. M., Cambron-McCabe, N., Lucas, T., Smith, B., Dutton, J., & Kleiner, A. (2000). *Schools that learn: A fifth discipline: Field book for educators, parents, and everyone who cares about education.* New York: Doubleday.

Sergiovanni, T. J. (1994). *Building community in schools.* San Francisco: Jossey-Bass.

Vygotsky, L. S. (1962). *Thought and language.* Cambridge, MA: MIT Press.

Vygotsky, L. S. (1978). *Mind in society.* Cambridge, MA: Harvard University Press.

Wheatley, M. J. (1992). *Leadership and the new science.* San Francisco: Berrett-Koehler.

Whitmore, J. (1996). *Coaching for performance.* Sonoma, CA: Nicholas Brealey.

Wolf, K. (1991). The school teacher's portfolio: Issues in design implementation, and evaluation. *Phi Delta Kappan, 73,* 129–136.

Wolf, K., & Dietz, M. (1998). Teaching portfolios: Purposes and possibilities. *Teacher Education Quarterly, 25*(1), 9–22.

Zemelman, S., Daniels, H., & Hyde, A. (1993). *Best practice: New standards for teaching and learning in America's schools.* Portsmouth, NH: Heinemann.

Index

CORWIN PRESS

The Corwin Press logo—a raven striding across an open book—represents the union of courage and learning. Corwin Press is committed to improving education for all learners by publishing books and other professional development resources for those serving the field of PreK–12 education. By providing practical, hands-on materials, Corwin Press continues to carry out the promise of its motto: **"Helping Educators Do Their Work Better."**